WALKING IN CUMBRIA'S EDEN VALLEY

About the Author

Vivienne Crow is a freelance writer and photographer specialising in the outdoors. A journalist since 1990, she abandoned the constraints of a desk job with regional newspapers in 2001 to go travelling in Asia and New Zealand. On her return, she decided to focus on the activities she loves the most: hill-walking, writing, travelling and photography. Needless to say, she's never looked back!

Based in Cumbria for the past 15 years, she has written seven books on the county, mostly walking guides, and is well-known in north Cumbria for her hugely popular walking columns, which appear in several local newspapers. She also writes outdoor features for magazines and does a lot of work for conservation and tourism bodies, researching and writing walks leaflets and interpretation panels.

Vivienne is assistant secretary of the Outdoor Writers and Photographers Guild.

Website: www.viviennecrow.co.uk

WALKING IN CUMBRIA'S EDEN VALLEY

by

Vivienne Crow

2 POLICE SQUARE, MILNTHORPE, CUMBRIA LA7 7PY
www.cicerone.co.uk

Printed in China on behalf of Latitude Press Ltd
Photographs by the author unless stated
A catalogue record for this book is available from the British Library.

Ordnance Survey This project includes mapping data licensed from Ordnance Survey® with the permission of the Controller of Her Majesty's Stationery Office. © Crown copyright 2011. All rights reserved. Licence number PU100012932

Acknowledgements

Charlie Emmett's book *The Eden Way* and John Wyatt's *Cumbria* proved invaluable while researching this guide; and Val Corbett's work, particularly her beautiful photographic collection *A Year in the Life of the Eden Valley*, was a constant source of inspiration.

The author also wishes to thank the following: Andrew Nicholson at Carlisle City Council; Gillian Luscombe and John Ballard at Cumbria County Council; Julie Darroch and Nicola Hewitson at Cumbria Tourism; the ever friendly and helpful assistants in the Eden Valley's tourist information centres; the team at Cicerone, always efficient, knowledgeable and ready to answer even my silliest of queries; Mark Richards for the voice of experience; the former team at the now defunct East Cumbria Countryside Project for all their hard work paving the way, so to speak, in the Eden Valley, in particular David Nightingale, Dick Capel and Marilyn Leech for all their encouragement when I worked with them on the Discover Eden project; and, most of all, Heleyne for her seemingly infinite patience.

Front cover: Maulds Meaburn is one of the many gorgeous villages in the Eden Valley

CONTENTS

Advice to Readers

Readers are advised that, while every effort is made by our authors to ensure the accuracy of guidebooks as they go to print, changes can occur during the lifetime of an edition. Please check Updates on this book's page on the Cicerone website (www.cicerone.co.uk) before planning your trip. We would also advise that you check information about such things as transport, accommodation and shops locally. Even rights of way can be altered over time. We are always grateful for information about any discrepancies between a guidebook and the facts on the ground, sent by email to info@cicerone.co.uk or by post to Cicerone, 2 Police Square, Milnthorpe LA7 7PY, United Kingdom.

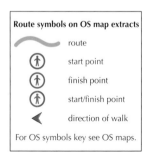

Route symbols on OS map extracts	
~~	route
🚶	start point
🚶	finish point
🚶	start/finish point
◄	direction of walk
For OS symbols key see OS maps.	

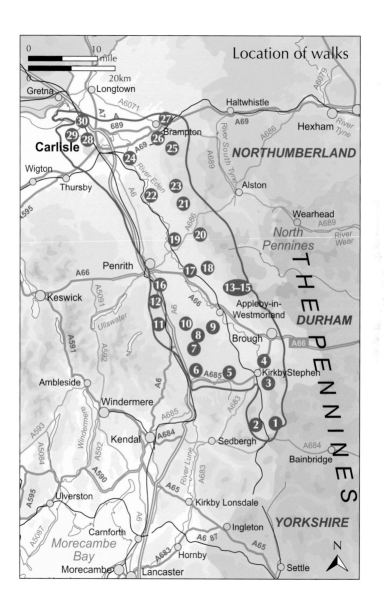

Autumn comes to Cumbria

INTRODUCTION

The River Eden near Langwathby with the radar station on Great Dun Fell visible in the background

THE EDEN VALLEY

If Cumbria's beautiful Eden Valley were anywhere but right next to the Lake District, it would be full of tourists. In reality, few venture this far from the National Park, leaving locals to delight in the fact that they have this wonderful area – with its rich natural and human heritage and its beautiful and diverse landscapes – all to themselves.

From its source high up on the wild moorlands of the North Pennines to the open spaces of the immense Solway marshes on the Scottish border, the River Eden meanders its way north for 75 wonderful miles. In terms of human history, geology, habitats, wildlife and landscape walkers could not wish for more variety within such a compact area. Bronze Age settlements, Roman forts and Celtic kingdoms, ruined castles, fortified churches and memories of Bonnie Prince Charlie – the Eden Valley has it all. The landscape alters with every twist and turn of the river – limestone pavement, peaty moorlands and the dramatic Whin Sill of High Cup spread out beside rolling pastures, red sandstone gorges and vast salt-marshes. And walkers are never short of company from the elusive black grouse, endangered red squirrels and shy otters to huge flocks of noisy waders.

Straddling the river, although not strictly within the area locals refer to as the 'Eden Valley', the largest settlement is the great border city of Carlisle, with its fascinating and often bloody history, changing from English control to Scottish and back again countless times. The attractive market towns of Kirkby Stephen, Appleby-in-Westmorland, Penrith and Brampton also have tons of character and are well worth visiting in their own right. They are built mostly from the red sandstone that gives this area such a distinctive look – as are the villages, hamlets, isolated farmhouses and fortified homes that dot the valley and creep up to the very base of the Pennines.

And then there are those views! Wherever you walk in the Eden Valley the Pennines, particularly Cross Fell, dominate the scenery, and you can also see across to the eastern edge of the Lake District, with Kidsty Pike and Blencathra often standing out on the horizon. As you make your way further downstream, towards the Solway Firth, the Scottish hills begin to appear in the distance: just a dreamy blue outline at first, but then with individual tops becoming more easily identifiable as you head further north.

As well as covering the valley of River Eden itself, this book includes walks in the valleys carved by some of its main tributaries, including the River Lowther, which runs just within the boundaries of the Lake District National Park, the River Lyvennet, the Eamont near Penrith and the lovely Gelt. And let's not forget the smaller streams too, sometimes just as dramatic and beautiful as their larger siblings such as Scandal Beck, Hoff Beck, Augill Beck, Raven Beck and many more.

The River Ure with Wild Boar Fell in the distance

GEOLOGY

The geology of the Eden Valley is complex, and the experts inevitably interpret it in several different ways. In simple terms, the underlying rock type changes as you move down the hillsides and closer to the river itself, and there are changes too as the river heads downstream.

The River Eden begins its life on the watershed of the high boggy moorlands of the North Pennines. The bedrock here, as in most of the North Pennines and the eastern Lake District fells, is of ancient Ordovician types, laid down by sedimentary processes more than 450 million years ago. These would have started life as a mush of black mud on the sea bed that was then hardened and compressed as the North American and European tectonic plates converged.

The young river, dropping through Hell Gill, quickly leaves the high ground and swings north to enter the narrow glacial valley of Mallerstang. The most noticeable rock type here is carboniferous limestone, capped by broken millstone grit escarpments.

Limestone is an important feature of the Upper Eden Valley, with many tributaries starting life on the pretty grasslands that are characteristic of this rock type. About 350 million years ago this area would have been covered by a tropical sea that was teeming with life. As generation after generation of these ocean creatures died, their shells formed a thick layer of sediment on the sea bed. This became the pale grey limestone that can be seen just breaking the surface along Lady Anne's Way in Mallerstang or, more obviously, forming large areas of Karst scenery including

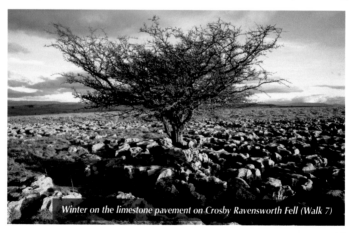

Winter on the limestone pavement on Crosby Ravensworth Fell (Walk 7)

11

limestone pavement on Great Asby Scar.

Limestone pavement is the result of the interplay of the soluble nature of the rock and the work of glaciers. About 2.6 million years ago the Earth began to cool, resulting in the formation of glaciers that covered huge areas of land with massive ice sheets. Although this tends to be called the 'Ice Age', within this Ice Age there were cold periods (glacials) and warmer periods (inter-glacials) when forests thrived. There were many of these temperature fluctuations, but it is the last cold period, which ended about 10,000 years ago, that has had the most profound effect on the Cumbrian landscape we see today.

The creation of limestone pavement began as the glaciers scoured the rock and ice and fractured it along existing horizontal lines of weakness known as bedding planes. Over time, water has been exploiting the bedding planes and other cracks in the limestone, slowly eroding and dissolving the rock. This has created the fascinating pattern of blocks (clints) and fissures (grikes) that we see today.

One of the most noticeable characteristics of the area closer to the River Eden itself, particularly in its middle reaches, is the new red sandstone. Churches, castles, farms and villages are all built from this distinctive rock, which positively glows as the sun dips towards the horizon at the end of a long summer evening. It does not require a huge leap of the imagination to envisage the desert conditions that created these rocks

Typical red sandstone cottages in Edenhall

Wildflower meadow

between the Permian period (280 million years ago) and the beginning of the Triassic (240 million years ago). At this time, what we now call Britain was lying just north of the Equator. Brockram, a breccia visible in the bed of the Eden near Kirkby Stephen, is the oldest of these desert rocks; the new red sandstone is slightly younger.

Hot arid conditions continued into the early part of the Triassic period, but by now seasonal rivers and shallow seas existed too, leaving mudstone deposits known today as the Eden shales. Later still in the Triassic, about 200 million years ago, the Mercia mudstones were deposited. These impervious rocks are found in the lower stretches of the river, near Carlisle.

WILDLIFE AND HABITATS

The plants, animals and birds that thrive in the Eden Valley are as varied as the area's geology and its resulting landscapes. Of course, here as in all parts of the UK, human beings have had a profound influence, but that is not to say that walkers will not have some fascinating, sometimes even rare, company as they enjoy the routes in this book.

The North Pennines, seemingly bleak and barren at first glance, contain some very important ecosystems. Almost 30 per cent of England's blanket bog is found here, home to peat-building sphagnum moss as well as heather, bog asphodel, crowberry and cotton grass. Rare Alpine plants, such as cloudberry, still thrive on the highest moors.

13

This locale, designated as an Area of Outstanding Natural Beauty, also contains 40 per cent of the UK's remaining 1100 hectares of upland hay meadows, which burst into life every spring and summer. An amazing tapestry of wild flowers blooms, filling the landscape with vivid colour, from the white of the early flowering wood anemone in March right up until October, when the purple of devil's bit scabious is having its final fling. There can be more than 30 different species growing in every square metre of hay meadow, and up to a hundred in any one field, providing a habitat for insects, birds and small mammals such as the increasingly rare water vole.

The moorlands and hay meadows are important for a variety of bird species including red grouse, some of England's last remaining populations of the elusive black grouse, the heavily persecuted and extremely rare hen harrier, merlin, short-eared owl, skylark, lapwing, golden plover, dunlin, twite, whinchat and wheatear. In spring and early summer the long bubbling song of the curlew may be heard. Having spent the winter on the coast, they and other wading birds move inland in the spring to breed. They particularly favour the rough, rushy allotments above the valley floor and the long grass of the meadows for nesting.

As far as mammals go, the most common species you are likely to see on the uplands is sheep, but there is wildlife too; foxes, hares and stoats can be seen, particularly around dusk and dawn, and further west in the eastern Lake District herds of red deer roam above the tree line. The valleys and low-lying woods are home to badgers, roe deer, voles, shrews, the occasional otter and, of course, red squirrels, sadly threatened by the encroachment of greys into this, one of their last bastions in England. Herons, kingfishers and dippers can often be spotted along the becks and rivers, and the woods are home to wagtails, long-tailed tits, great spotted woodpeckers, cuckoos, siskins, redpolls, finches and warblers among others. Buzzards are probably the most common of the raptors, but small numbers of ospreys, peregrine falcons and, increasingly, red kites can sometimes also be seen.

The limestone grasslands are a delight for amateur botanists. Hoary rock-rose, lily-of-the-valley and many rare orchids can be found on the limestone pavement. In the early summer these areas are full of colour, not only thanks to the vast array of flora but also because of the butterflies that breed here: brimstones, dark green fritillaries, graylings and common blues along with some of England's rarest species such as the Scotch argus.

Having risen on the edge of the North Pennines Area of Outstanding Natural Beauty, the River Eden ends its journey at the Solway Coast Area of Outstanding Natural Beauty, another ecologically important locale. This low-lying area includes a wide range

Criffel, in Dumfries and Galloway, is visible on the other side of the Solway Firth

of fragile ecosystems, including raised mires, sand dunes, mudflats and salt-marshes. Where the waters of the Eden slowly turn brackish, wild flowers such as marsh samphire (or glass-wort), pennywort and sea thrift thrive. Every winter the entire population of barnacle geese from the Svalbard archipelago in the Arctic Ocean descends on the English and Scottish marshes of the Solway Firth: between 25,000 and 30,000 birds, impressive both to see and hear. Thousands of other swans, ducks and geese also take advantage of the relatively mild Solway winters, as do snow bunting, twite and glaucous and Iceland gulls. The Solway is also a major migration route for seabirds such as the pomarine skua in the spring and shearwaters and storm petrels in late summer.

HISTORY

The River Eden flows through the old counties of Westmorland and Cumberland which, during the 1974 local government reorganisation, were brought together and combined with parts of Lancashire and Yorkshire to form the modern county of Cumbria. But that does not mean the 'new' county was simply dreamt up by 20th-century bureaucrats; the word 'Cumbria' has its origins in the Celtic words *Cymri* or *Cumber*, meaning 'brothers' or 'countrymen', and the borders of modern-day Cumbria roughly equate to those of the Celtic kingdom of Rheged.

It is thought that people probably first made an appearance in what is today called Cumbria towards the end of the last Ice Age, but these

Palaeolithic hunters did not venture very far north. There is evidence too of Mesolithic people, but it was really only in Neolithic times that humans began to make their mark on the region. Up until then Mother Nature had been in charge of sculpting the landscape and clothing it as she saw fit, but the late Stone Age heralded a massive revolution as humans began to settle and farm. Neolithic people created clearings in the forests to build their settlements and grow crops, and they used the forests as a wood and timber resource and as grazing and browsing for their livestock.

The arrival of the 'Beaker' people in the Eden Valley early in the second millennium BC heralded the start of the Bronze Age. This period is associated with some of the most enigmatic of prehistoric remains: stone circles such as Long Meg and the henge at Mayburgh. The next group of 'off-comers' to arrive were the Celts in about 300BC. These Iron Age people were more sophisticated; they introduced advanced mixed farming techniques to the region as well as their language – a predecessor of modern Welsh. Many of the names of the county's topographical features are Celtic in origin; for example, *blain,* meaning summit, gives rise to 'blen' as in Blencarn.

The Romans arrived in Britain in AD43 and at first the Celts co-operated with the new rulers, living autonomously in their northern kingdom. However, when the Celtic tribes began fighting among themselves the Romans became increasingly involved

Looking across to Talkin Fell

in the affairs of this remote corner of the empire. But they clearly never saw it as a good place in which to live; it was purely a military zone, and as such there are no villas or markets or even Roman place names, just roads, forts, such as the one at Brougham, and other defensive structures.

The conquerors finally left this far north-western outpost to itself in AD410. So began the Dark Ages, a period when fact and fiction became intertwined and semi-mythological figures such as King Arthur and Urien of Rheged appeared. The armies of the north were commanded by Cole Hen, who became king following the Romans' departure – probably the 'Old King Cole' of the nursery rhyme. On his death his huge kingdom was carved up by his descendants. One of these was Urien who ruled sixth-century Rheged from his supposed base near modern-day Crosby Ravensworth.

The power of the Celts began to decline in the early seventh century and before long the Anglo-Saxons were the dominant force in much of lowland Cumbria. Their influence can be seen in place names such as Clifton (meaning farmstead on the hill) and in the intricately carved crosses such as the one at St Michael and All Angels Church, Addingham. The uplands, meanwhile, were being settled by pastoralist Vikings who had come from Norway via Ireland and the Isle of Man. Like the Anglo-Saxons, they too left their carved stone emblems, including the Loki Stone in the church at Kirkby Stephen, and remnants of their language. Look at a modern map of Norway and you will quickly discover why the Cumbrians call their hills and mountains fells – *fjell* means 'mountain' in Norwegian. The Norse word for waterfall is *foss*, which becomes 'force' in the Eden Valley, *tjorn* becomes 'tarn', *dalr* becomes 'dale' and *bekkr* 'beck'.

The Normans' Harrying of the North in 1069–70 resulted in a high death toll and the destruction of much of the region's cultivable land, but it wasn't until 1092, when William Rufus decided to build a castle at Carlisle, that the invaders began to take an interest in more direct control of the population. The son of William the Conqueror, William Rufus brought in English settlers who owed their allegiance to the Normans and he divided the region up among his barons, who built several castles in the Eden Valley.

Throughout the 12th century and the early part of the 13th century the stronghold of Carlisle passed from Scottish to English hands and back again several times. It was not until 1216 that the English finally gained control and, except for a brief interlude when Bonnie Prince Charlie captured the city in 1745, it has remained in English hands ever since. But that is not to say that these border regions were forever peaceful after 1216. In fact, Edward I's determination to impose English sovereignty on Scotland marked a resurgence in border difficulties, which continued long after his death at Burgh by Sands in 1307. In the early part of the 14th century Scottish raiders, led by Robert the Bruce, ransacked much of the north of the county and the villages of the Eden Valley. Towns were burned, churches destroyed and villagers slaughtered. It was a truly grim century for the area, which also had to cope with famines and the Black Death. And, as if all that was not enough, the period from the 13th century to the middle of the 17th was also the time of the Border Reivers – the clans that regularly carried out cross-border raids, looting and pillaging and bringing new, bleak words to the English language such as 'bereaved' and 'blackmail'. In this period of great instability the fear and insecurity engendered by these bloody times is reflected in the buildings of the era. Churches, such as the one at Burgh by Sands, were fortified and wealthy families built themselves stout sturdy refuges, known as Pele towers, next to their homes.

Cumberland and Westmorland were slow to pick up on the changes that swept the rest of England during the Agricultural Revolution, partly because of their isolation and partly because the hilly landscape made their circumstances very different from those in the arable south. Drystone walls, still a very important feature of the Eden Valley today, first started appearing from about 1750. Snaking up and down even the steepest of fellsides, these 'enclosures' were stimulated mostly by rising food

Drystone walls are a significant feature of the countryside

prices, which encouraged farmers to reclaim wasteland and commons. Of course, the region did eventually catch up, and agriculture is now a crucial element of the modern local economy.

If the region was a little slow to join the Agricultural Revolution, it was one of the first in line when it came to the Industrial Revolution. In the North Pennines lead mining was providing employment for hundreds of people, and the area's wealth of water, in the form of fast-flowing rivers and becks, allowed it to play a significant role in the textile industry, either by providing bobbins for the huge mills of Lancashire and Yorkshire or, in the case of the Carlisle area, by joining the big boys in the making of cloth.

The coming of the railways was one of the main catalysts for industrial development on such a massive scale. Cumbria's first public railway, connecting Carlisle with Newcastle, was completed in 1838, but it was in the 1840s that what we know today as the West Coast Main Line first sliced through the Lune Gorge, up and over the 914ft Shap Summit and on to Carlisle. Then, in 1876, came the Settle–Carlisle Railway, England's last navvy-built line.

WEATHER

There is no denying that Cumbria is a wet county – Borrowdale in the Lake District holds the UK record for the highest rainfall in a 24-hour period – but that really is only a tiny fraction of the overall picture. The Eden Valley is protected from the worst of the prevailing south-westerly air flows bringing the wind and rain by the mountains of the Lake District and it is therefore slightly drier than much of the county. Even when it does rain, the cloud does not normally hang around for long. If you spend a week in the Eden Valley, you would be unlucky if you had more than one day of constant rainfall; more likely, you will get a few days of sunshine and showers and one or two days of brilliant blue skies. And that applies whatever the time of year. Of course there are some months that tend to be drier than others; early spring and late autumn often hold some pleasant surprises, but don't expect August to be drier than November; it just doesn't work like that in Cumbria.

The wonderful thing about the climate here is that the sky and the quality of the light are ever-changing. You can stand on Cross Fell, the roof of the Pennines, and see curtains of showers coming in from the west, look to the north and the Scottish hills will be bathed in sunshine under a cloudless sky, turn round and there are bruised purple storm clouds gathering over County Durham and Northumberland. It's never boring!

As far as temperatures go, Cumbria tends to be cooler than the south of England, but the warming effect of the North Atlantic Drift

Cross Fell, the highest point on the Pennines, towers over the Eden Valley

keeps the mercury above the levels experienced on the eastern side of the Pennines. It also receives regular snowfall, particularly in January and February. This tends to be confined to the higher fells, but the Pennine roads and more isolated valley routes can often become blocked. Cross Fell is often the first county top to receive a dusting of snow, sometimes as early as mid-October, and it is also the last to lose its white covering, which can linger well into May.

The weather may not be a crucial factor when doing the low-level walks in this book, but it is an important consideration if you are intending to head on to the open moors. Make sure you get an accurate, mountain-specific weather forecast before setting out. The Lake District forecast provided by the Mountain Weather Information

Service (www.mwis.org.uk) covers the whole of Cumbria and the western Pennines north of Ingleborough.

The Helm Wind

The North Pennines and Eden Valley are home to Britain's only named wind. Not unlike the famous *föhn* wind of the Alps, the howling helm wind occurs when a north-easterly air flow hits the Pennine escarpment near Cross Fell. The air climbs the eastern slopes and then comes hurtling down the western side at full pelt, meeting the warmer air from the west as it does so. The result is a ferocious easterly wind that lasts for days and can be felt all the way from Brough to Brampton. A visible sign of the wind is the bank of cloud that forms just above the fell-tops, sometimes covering Cross Fell. This is known as the 'helm cloud' or simply the 'helm'. Another bank of cloud, known as the 'helm bar' sometimes forms parallel to the helm cloud.

A particularly strange, slightly disturbing aspect of the helm is the way that just a few miles to the west of the fellside settlements the wind simply dies. You can stand in Penrith without a hint of a breeze and listen to the roar of the helm wind to the east.

WHERE TO STAY

There is a good range of both self-catering and bed and breakfast accommodation throughout the Eden Valley. Most towns and villages have a number of guesthouses, hotels and inns, and there are also plenty of more isolated farmhouse B&Bs scattered throughout the area. Prices tend to be slightly lower than in the neighbouring Lake District, but the quality is often just as high. Visitor numbers are higher during the school holidays, but you are unlikely to experience any problems finding somewhere to stay, although Appleby becomes rather busy during the horse fair at the beginning of June each year.

For budget travellers, there are YHA hostels at Kirkby Stephen and Dufton, the former a stopping-off point for walkers doing Wainwright's Coast to Coast walk, and the latter being popular with back-packers on the Pennine Way. If you are looking for somewhere to pitch your tent then www.ukcampsite.co.uk is a good place to start your search.

Kirkby Stephen, Appleby, Armathwaite and Carlisle are probably the best bases for the walks in this book, particularly if you are relying on public transport, but Crosby

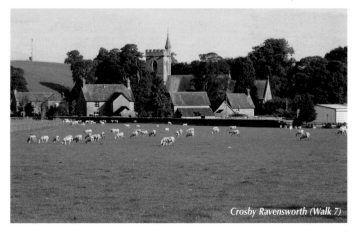

Crosby Ravensworth (Walk 7)

21

Ravensworth, Dufton, Penrith, Kirkoswald, Wetheral and Brampton are also very pleasant and interesting places to stay. If you are having a break from the walking there are castles, ruined abbeys, picturesque churches, gardens and nature reserves to visit. The border city of Carlisle is well worth a trip in its own right; the medieval castle and beautiful cathedral both have fascinating histories, and the award-winning Tullie House Museum and Art Gallery contains lots of cleverly designed exhibits that tell the fascinating story of the city in an interesting and accessible way.

The local Tourist Information Centres, listed in Appendix B, are a good place to start your search for accommodation. The staff are normally both friendly and knowledgeable. Cumbria Tourism's website also contains a wide selection of properties: www.golakes.co.uk. Don't be put off by the name; it covers the whole of Cumbria.

GETTING AROUND

The Eden Valley and nearby towns are surprisingly well served in terms of the national rail network. The West Coast Main Line, linking London Euston with Glasgow, passes through east Cumbria. All trains stop at Carlisle, and some also stop at Penrith North Lakes. With large stretches of the line capable of handling trains travelling at speeds of up to 125mph, it is now possible to travel the 310 miles from London to Carlisle in as little as 3hrs 12mins. The journey time from Glasgow to Carlisle is about 1hr 10mins.

Carlisle, Wetheral and Brampton are on the line to Newcastle with trains roughly every hour. The journey time

Remote Garsdale Station

from Newcastle to Carlisle is about 1hr 25mins. There are also about six trains a day from Leeds to Carlisle (journey time 2hrs 45mins). This journey is made via the scenic Settle–Carlisle railway, famously saved from the axe in the 1980s. Trains on this line also stop at various points throughout the Eden Valley, including Armathwaite, Lazonby, Langwathby, Appleby-in-Westmorland, Kirkby Stephen and, just outside the area, remote Garsdale. Inevitably, it is a popular line with walkers, and several of the linear routes in this guide make use of it.

National Express runs several daily services from London to Carlisle (average journey time 7hrs). There are also at least six coaches every day linking Carlisle with Glasgow (journey time 2hrs), Manchester (3hrs 15mins) and Birmingham International Airport (5hrs). National Express also has a

daily service between Inverness and London Victoria that stops in Penrith (journey time to London 6hrs 10mins).

Outside of the main towns the area is poorly served by local buses. Looking at a route map for the area east of the Eden there may appear to be lots of services, but look again and you will see that most of these are Fellrunner buses that operate just once a week, twice if you're lucky. Although listed in the 'transport' section for each walk, they are of little practical use to walkers.

For information on bus and rail routes and timetables, phone Traveline on 0871 200 2233 or visit the website, www.traveline.org.uk.

WAYMARKING AND ACCESS

Most of the walks in this guide make use of the superb network

An unusual stile beside the Lyvennet (Walk 8)

of public rights of way in the Eden Valley. Although some of the paths and bridleways are surprisingly little used, particularly across farmland and through pleasant riverside meadows, they are generally well signposted and a succession of sturdy gates and stiles guide the way. Walkers have the former East Cumbria Countryside Project to thank for much of the work that has been done in recent years on waymarking, maintaining path furniture and opening up new routes. Sadly, the organisation no longer exists, a victim of budget cuts.

A few of the walks also cross areas of open moorland that have been designated 'access land' under the Countryside and Rights of Way Act 2000. This Act gave people the right to walk across land thus designated on maps – mostly mountains, moor, heath and common land – without having to stick to rights of way. Although most areas are open all of the time, restrictions can be imposed to protect wildlife, farm livestock and the public for up to 28 days a year, for example, when grouse shooting is taking place. Dogs are allowed in some areas as long as they are under close control, but they may be banned entirely from some moorland. From 1 March to 31 July they should be kept on a 2m lead to protect ground-nesting birds.

Information on access land restrictions and closures is usually posted at major access points, but you can check in advance on the Natural England website, www.natural england.org.uk.

Eden Benchmarks

Walkers will come across some interesting art projects as they wander the paths of the Eden Valley. One of these is the Eden Benchmarks, a series of sculptures commissioned by the East Cumbria Countryside Project to celebrate the new millennium. Each by a different artist, they have

Water Cut, the first of the Eden Benchmarks

been installed at various locations beside public paths along the entire length of the River Eden. Each also functions as a seat. The artists' brief was to produce sculptures that harmonised with the landscape and captured the essence of each locality. The first is *Water Cut* by Mary Bourne, located high on the wild moorland close to the source of the river at Mallerstang. The other nine are at Kirkby Stephen, Temple Sowerby, Appleby, Lazonby, Edenhall, Armathwaite, Wetheral, Bitts Park in Carlisle and Rockcliffe, close to the mouth of the river.

MAPS

The map extracts used in this book are taken from the Ordnance Survey's 1:50,000 Landranger series. They are meant as a guide only and walkers are advised to purchase the relevant map(s), and know how to navigate using them, before setting off. The whole area is covered by sheets 85, 86, 90, 91 and 98.

The OS 1:25,000 Explorer series provides greater detail, showing field boundaries as well as the extent of access land. To complete all the walks in this guide using Explorer maps, you will need sheets 315, OL5, OL31 and OL19.

CLOTHING, EQUIPMENT AND SAFETY

The amount of gear you carry with you on a walk and the clothes you choose to wear will differ according to the length of the walk, the time of year and the terrain you are likely to encounter. Preparing for the 17-mile hike across the exposed moorland above Mallerstang requires considerably more thought than when setting out on a 3¼-mile Sunday morning stroll from Armathwaite. As such, this section is aimed at those heading out in the winter or venturing on to the higher ground; summer or valley walkers should adjust their kit accordingly.

Even in the height of summer, your daysack should contain everything you need to make yourself wind- and waterproof. Most people will also carry a few extra layers of clothing; this is more important if you are heading on to higher ground where the weather can be unpredictable and prone to sudden change. As far as footwear goes, some walkers like good, solid leather boots with plenty of ankle support while others prefer something lighter. Whatever you wear, make sure it has a good grip and is unlikely to result in a twisted ankle on uneven ground. You may also consider investing in gaiters, particularly if you are hoping to walk several of the Pennine routes, where it can be boggy.

Every walker needs to carry a map and compass, and know how to use them. Always carry sufficient food and water to sustain you during the walk and provide extra emergency rations in case you are out for longer than you originally planned. Emergency equipment should include a whistle and a torch, the distress signal being six flashes/whistle-blasts repeated at 1min intervals. Pack a small first aid kit too.

Carry a fully charged mobile phone, just in case of a genuine emergency. If things do go badly wrong and you need help, first make sure you have a note of all the relevant details such as your location, the nature of the injury or problem, the number of people in the party and your mobile phone number. Only then should you dial 999 and ask for the police, then mountain rescue.

Walkers should also remember that, as with anywhere in the country, the waterside paths used in this guidebook might become waterlogged or even flooded after periods of exceptional rain. Some parts of Burgh and

Rockcliffe marshes (Walks 29 and 30) may also become inundated at times of particularly high tides.

Mobile phone coverage is generally fine in the Eden Valley, although it can be patchy in Mallerstang and some more isolated villages. The signal tends to be good on higher ground.

USING THIS GUIDE

The routes in this book are designed to give the walker a taste of everything the Eden Valley has to offer. From peaceful woodland strolls to serious moorland hikes, and from explorations of the limestone uplands to walks on the Solway marshes, they visit just about every nook and cranny of this beautiful area. The walks also take in many of the river's tributaries, just straying on a couple of occasions

Woodland beside the River Petteril, a tributary of the River Eden

The edge of Talkin Fell is guarded by a line of tall cairns

into the Lake District National Park. Ullswater, Patterdale and the parts of the Northern Fells that also fall into the Eden catchment, however, have been deliberately missed out because they are already covered by scores of walking guides to the Lake District.

The walks are ordered from source to sea, starting from the head of the river in the south and gradually working their way north to where the Eden meets the Solway Firth. Most of the routes are circular, but there are a few linear walks that make use of the area's regular rail services, including the Settle–Carlisle line. Check timetables carefully, especially on longer walks, to make sure you have enough time to complete the route.

Each walk is graded one to five, one being the easiest, but please note that these ratings are subjective, and walkers are advised to read the route description before setting out to gain a better understanding of what to expect. It may be a good idea to do an easy walk first and then judge the rest accordingly. There is a route summary table at the back of the book in Appendix A to help you find a route quickly that meets your requirements.

WALK 1

Mallerstang and Nine Standards

Distance	17 miles (27.2km)
Total ascent	912m (2990ft)
Start	Garsdale railway station (SD 788 917)
Finish	Kirkby Stephen railway station (NY 761 067)
Terrain	Good bridleways and tracks and open moorland, boggy in places
Walking time	9hrs
Grade	5
Maps	OS Explorer OL19 or OS Landranger 98 and 91
Transport	The start and finish are both on the Settle–Carlisle railway
Refreshments	Moorcock Inn, Garsdale Head; variety of pubs and cafés in Kirkby Stephen

Mallerstang is a remote valley on the Cumbria–North Yorkshire border, the point at which the River Eden emerges from its peaty source on Black Fell Moss, plummets down through Hell Gill and begins its long journey north to the Solway Firth. This route, which follows high ground to the east of the valley, is the longest, toughest walk in this guidebook, but it is worth every ounce of effort. Interesting limestone features, grand views of three counties, a sense of history, expansive moorland and a wonderful feeling of remoteness are the order of the day.

Leave Garsdale Station, turn right along the minor road and, immediately after the cottages, go through the smaller of two gates on the right. This new stretch of gravel bridleway leads to the **A684**. Cross straight over to continue along the bridleway and then do the same at the next road, just behind the **Moorcock Inn**.

THE SETTLE–CARLISLE RAILWAY

The Settle–Carlisle Railway was the last mainline railway in England to be constructed almost entirely by hand. Carving its convoluted route through the Pennines, it was a major feat of engineering and the statistics bear this out. Work on the 72-mile line began in 1869 and lasted for seven years. The line opened to passengers on 1 May 1876 and includes 14 tunnels and more than 20 viaducts. The Ribblehead Viaduct is 400m long and 100ft above the ground. The longest tunnel, Blea Moor, is 2404m long. About 6000 men were involved in building it. Many workers were injured or killed during the construction, and many more died through outbreaks of smallpox and other diseases which spread quickly in the makeshift, unhygienic settlements in which they lived.

The line has famously survived two attempts to close it: once in the early 1960s and again in the 1980s.

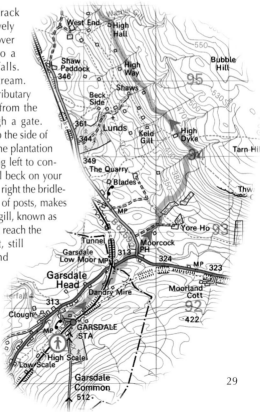

Turn right at the track junction to cross the lovely old humpback bridge over the River Ure, close to a series of small waterfalls. Turn left, heading upstream. Shortly after fording a tributary beck bear right, away from the main track and through a gate. Climb the rough track up the side of Cobbles Plantation. As the plantation fence swings right, swing left to continue uphill with a small beck on your right. As the beck swings right the bridleway, marked by a series of posts, makes its way over to a fenced gill, known as Johnston Gill. When you reach the beck, swing sharp right, still following the posts, and go through the gate at the top of the enclosure. Turn left along the clear track.

Having followed the High Way for about 3.5km, cross the high-sided

29

The view from Lady Anne's Way is dominated by Wild Boar Fell across the valley

LADY ANNE'S WAY

Crossing several becks along the way, and passing a number of long-abandoned farms, always with Wild Boar Fell dominating the magnificent view across the valley, this track passes through some fascinating limestone country. Known as the High Way or Lady Anne's Way, it is said to be the route that Lady Anne Clifford used to take from her castle in Skipton to visit the Westmorland estates she inherited when she was 60. For more on Lady Anne's legacy, see Walk 4.

stone bridge over Hell Gill and turn right along a faint track immediately after the dark wooded ravine, heading north-east. This becomes clearer on the ground as you gently climb, ignoring any lesser paths off to the right. At first follow the line of **Hell Gill Beck** is over to the right. After about 1.2km the path swings north, making towards the edge of the escarpment and winding its way up to a cairn.

With steeper ground on the left, follow the escarpment edge northwards, ignoring a track off to the right soon after the cairn. After the dull, featureless plod up from Hell Gill, the edge of **Hangingstone Scar** will put the spring back in your step. As you gain height, Cumbria slowly reveals itself – Wild Boar Fell, the Lake District, the North Pennines – and the cliffs at your feet become quite dramatic. All too soon, it seems, the path swings away from the edge and makes its way towards the prominent cairn at **Gregory Chapel**. But there's no need to feel down-hearted because the route now follows the ridge proper, with views east and north-east far into North Yorkshire and County Durham.

Ignoring the small cairn to the right, head north along the clear ridge path, quickly crossing a small area strangely devoid of vegetation. At the next cairn bear right to head downhill. The path crosses a flat boggy area and then climbs to **High Seat** which, at 709m, is the highest point on the walk. Continuing north along the Cumbria–North Yorkshire border, the ridge route crosses increasingly boggy ground. If you lose the path, simply keep heading north. About 1km beyond High Seat you reach the cairn on **High Pike Hill** and, soon after this, the path makes a pronounced swing right (north-east) and begins to descend.

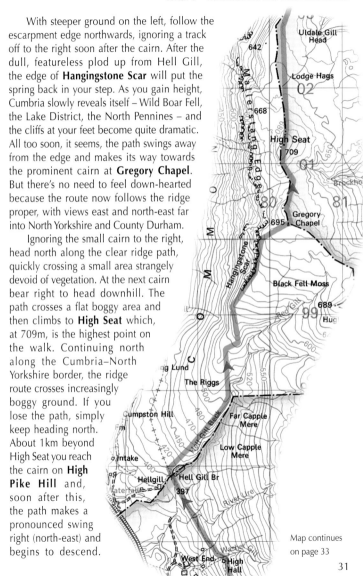

Map continues on page 33

31

Dukerdale

It winds its way down to a clear grassy track near some sinkholes. As you near the road turn right and head for the fingerpost beside the **B6270**.

Cross straight over to follow the wide grassy path northwards. Bear right at a fork. This path first heads north-east, swings north along the edge of eroded limestone pavement and then swings north-east again across some damp ground, making for the wall around Dukerdale. Approaching the head of this attractive limestone valley, join a track coming in from the left and ford a beck. The path climbs alongside the wall for a short while and then heads towards a prominent stone structure on high ground to the north-east. From here walk east along a clear path across the open moor towards a fingerpost. This indicates the route of the Coast to Coast, but ignore it and instead head north-eastwards. Climbing all the while, the faint track dissolves into the surrounding peat, but keep heading north-east to reach the viewpoint on **Nine Standards Rigg**. Turn left to reach the Nine Standards themselves.

The origin of the 'stone men' or tall cairns on Nine Standards Rigg is a mystery. One claim is that they were constructed by the Romans to look like troops from a distance; others say they are boundary markers. Major repairs on some of the cairns were carried out in 2005.

From the cairns, pick up a path heading west. The start of the well-walked route is marked by two tiny imitations of the stone men. Descend to a wall and turn right along an old miners' track. This clear track eventually

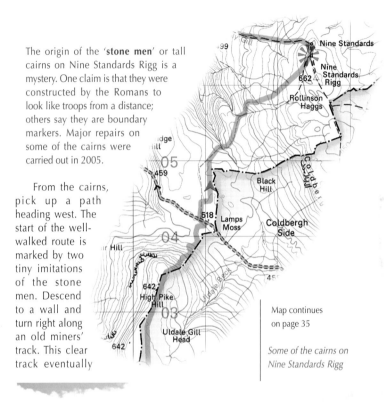

Map continues on page 35

Some of the cairns on Nine Standards Rigg

33

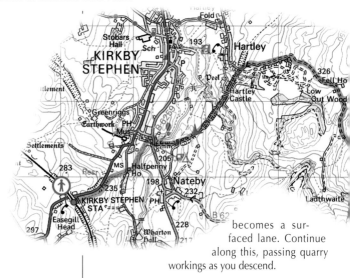

becomes a sur-
faced lane. Continue
along this, passing quarry
workings as you descend.

Hartley Quarry started operations in 1925, and work
there became a reserved occupation in World War II
because the limestone was used in the steel industry
and lime was needed to bring much-needed marginal
land into food production. Today it provides aggregate
for road building.

After 2.5km of road walking, watch for the entrance
to the railway path on your left. This is close to the main
entrance to the quarry. Go through the gate and follow
the disused railway for about 1km.

This track was once part of the **South Durham and
Lancashire Union Railway**. Most of the line was closed
in 1962, but this section linking Hartley Quarry with
Appleby remained open until 1975. In more recent
years it has been brought back into use as a path by the
Northern Viaduct Trust, which has also installed information panels explaining the history of the area. For
more information on the railway see Walk 5.

Just before passing under the **B6259 road bridge**, turn right to cross the Millennium Bridge over the River Eden. Ignoring two trails off to the right, follow the path to a gate. Go through and turn left along the road. Just before another bridge, go through the gate on the right. Descend the steps to regain the riverside path. Cross a stile and bear left along the grassy path, still following the river upstream but ignoring the faint trail along the riverbank itself. You soon join a fence on your left, and then cross a

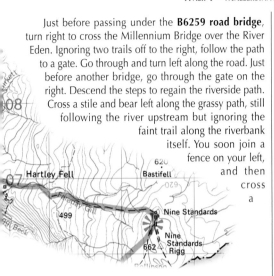

stile. Turn right and, quickly crossing yet another stile, follow the wall on your right and then go through the large gate to the left of **Halfpenny House**.

Turn right along the track and then immediately left before the cattle grid. Walk with the wall on your right, passing through a number of gates as you head uphill through several fields. Turn right along the **Kirkby Stephen railway station** access road and then left up the pedestrian slope leading to the platforms.

Waymarking tends to be good on most of the walks

35

WALK 2

Wild Boar Fell

Distance	12 miles (19.3km)
Total ascent	723m (2370ft)
Start	Garsdale railway station (SD 788 917)
Finish	Kirkby Stephen railway station (NY 761 067)
Terrain	Field paths, tracks and open moor, boggy in places
Walking time	7hrs
Grade	5
Maps	OS Explorer OL19 or OS Landranger 98 and 91
Transport	The start and finish are both on the Settle–Carlisle railway
Refreshments	Variety of pubs and cafés in Kirkby Stephen

Another wonderfully wild day on the hills above the upper Eden, this time on the western side of the valley. Ordnance Survey maps show no paths on lonely Swarth Fell (2234ft) and Wild Boar Fell (2322ft), but in reality there are routes on the ground and the walls and fences also aid navigation. Nonetheless, this walk is best saved for a clear day, if only to appreciate the magnificent views of the Howgills, the North Pennines and even the Lake District.

Leave Garsdale station and turn right along the minor road down to a T-junction with the **A684**. Cross over and go through a gate in the wall opposite. There isn't a clear path on the ground, but simply keep about 10m to the right of the wall and you will reach a small gate. Go through and continue in roughly the same direction.

Beyond the next gate, head along the grassy swathe towards Swarth Fell in the distance (NNW). About 75m after passing a farmhouse on your left, go through a gate on your left. A narrow grassy path heads north-west to pass through a gap in a wall about 50m to the left of a small barn. Continue in the same direction to reach another wall gap and then drop to a lane via some ruined buildings. ◄

This pretty spot is known as Grisedale, 'valley of the wild boar'.

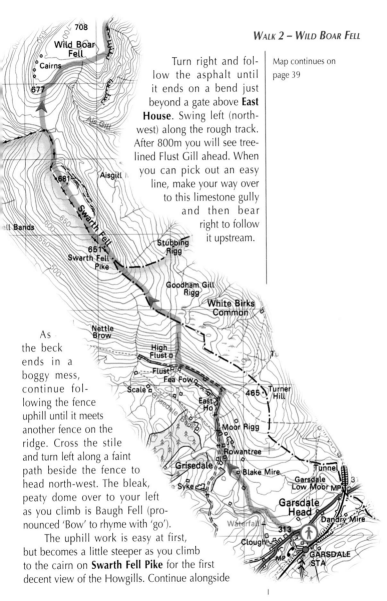

Turn right and fol-
low the asphalt until
it ends on a bend just
beyond a gate above **East
House**. Swing left (north-
west) along the rough track.
After 800m you will see tree-
lined Flust Gill ahead. When
you can pick out an easy
line, make your way over
to this limestone gully
and then bear
right to follow
it upstream.

Map continues on
page 39

As
the beck
ends in a
boggy mess,
continue fol-
lowing the fence
uphill until it meets
another fence on the
ridge. Cross the stile
and turn left along a faint
path beside the fence to
head north-west. The bleak,
peaty dome over to your left
as you climb is Baugh Fell (pronounced 'Bow' to rhyme with 'go').

The uphill work is easy at first,
but becomes a little steeper as you climb
to the cairn on **Swarth Fell Pike** for the first
decent view of the Howgills. Continue alongside

The grassy Howgill Fells can be seen to the west

You can now see right across the top of the Howgills to the Lake District.

the fence and then a wall to reach the highest point at the north-west end of this elongated summit. ◄

Follow the wall into the saddle between Swarth Fell and **Wild Boar Fell**. Here, as you pass a long thin tarn, the wall swings left. Continue straight on alongside the fence for the time being. About half-way up the next slope, bear right (north-east) at an indistinct fork. Instead of climbing to the trig point, this path hugs the escarpment edge, which it reaches near a line of tall cairns (not marked on the map).

As with so many Cumbrian fells, there is a legend behind the name '**Wild Boar**'. England's last wild boar, before the packs now roaming the south-west escaped from captivity, is said to have been killed on Wild Boar Fell by Sir Richard de Musgrave, who lived at Hartley Castle. A boar's tusk was later found in his tomb in Kirkby Stephen parish church.

If you thought the views were good up to this point, you're in for a treat now. Cross the stile in the fence and follow the faint path along the edge of the fell. Huge slabs of rock lie in piles at the foot of the crags to your right. More than 1300ft below the infant River Eden snakes it way through a magnificent valley at the start of its long journey to the Solway Firth. Further north, the valley widens as the river skirts the base of the highest of the Pennines, including Cross Fell.

Dropping from the summit area, you will reach a wall where you cross the route of a bridleway. Do not go through the gate; instead, continue in roughly the same direction, with the wall on your left. When the wall swings left, keep straight ahead (north) on a gently rising path that leads on to **Little Fell**. From the cairn at its northern end, quad bike tracks lead the way north across the open grassy fellside.

Soon after joining another wall, bear left at a fork up onto **Greenlaw Rigg**. Continue on the track down the ridge to a minor road and turn left. In about 100m as the road swings left, bear right along a faint track through the grass. Bear left at the wall and walk under the **railway**.

Beyond the gate you are channelled down to a farm track, along which you bear left, towards **Croop House**. Drawing level

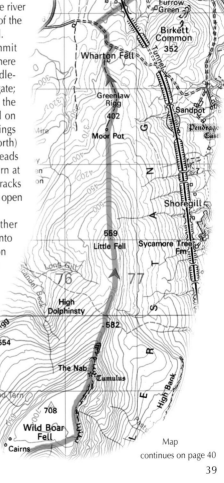

Map
continues on page 40

39

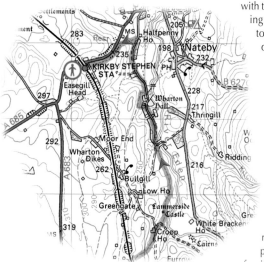

with the end of the last building on the left, bear right to follow a rough track down to a pair of gates. Go through the one on the left and climb to a gate to the right of the picturesque ruins of **Lammerside Castle**.

Lammerside Castle was built in the 12th century and was then strengthened in the 14th century to provide protection against Scottish raiders. It was occupied by the Wharton family, but they abandoned it in the 17th century, when they moved to the fortified manor house, Wharton Hall, which dates from the early 15th century.

There is a clear line through the crops here. It heads north and then swings north-east to go through a small gate in the field corner. Go through another gate opposite and then continue in the same direction. Once through the next gate, follow the fence on your right until the field narrows. Go through the large metal gate on your left and turn right along the concrete track. Ignore the turning on your right.

As you reach the buildings of **Wharton Hall**, take the track on the left. This quickly leads to a gate. Go through and turn right, walking parallel with a wall to the right. Go through a gate in another wall and head downhill, to the left of a large tree. A small gate provides access to a clear track, along which you turn left.

The track ends near **Halfpenny House**. Turn left just before the cattle grid. Walk with the wall on your right, passing through a number of gates as you head uphill through several fields. Turn right along the Kirkby Stephen station access road and then left up the pedestrian slope leading to the platforms.

WALK 3
The Infant Eden and Pendragon Castle

Distance	9 miles (14.3km)
Total ascent	346m (1135ft)
Start/finish	Parish church in Kirkby Stephen (NY 775 088)
Terrain	Field paths and tracks, low moorland
Walking time	4½ hrs
Grade	2
Maps	OS Explorer OL19 or OS Landranger 91
Transport	A bus serves Kirkby Stephen from Kendal. The walk also passes within 800m of Kirkby Stephen Station
Refreshments	Variety of pubs and cafés in Kirkby Stephen

This gentle walk starts from the attractive market town of Kirkby Stephen. It heads upstream alongside the River Eden as far as the romantic ruins of Pendragon Castle, passing some fascinating rock formations along the way and then entering more rugged country as the valley narrows. The return route heads for slightly higher ground before dropping back down to the Eden.

From the colonnaded entrance to Kirkby Stephen Parish Church, head south along the main road. Turn left at the traffic lights, towards Nateby. Keep going when the pavement runs out and then, immediately after a cottage on the left, bear left.

This is Kirkby Stephen's excellent **Poetry Path**, featuring 12 short poems by local poet Meg Peacocke, all beautifully carved into a series of stones. As people walk the path they progress through the farming year, each poem

One of the carved stones along the Poetry Path

depicting a different month. The first of the poems is at the end of this track.

Turn right along the riverside path. Before long, you reach a particularly interesting section of the river, where the water has carved the bedrock into weird and wonderful shapes. Keep to the main path as it briefly climbs away from the river and reaches a gate at the road.

It is worth taking a short detour to the **Millennium Bridge** by taking the path on your left before the gate. This provides a great view down into the gorge. The bedrock here is unusual; it is made of brockram, a mixture of limestone and sandstone fragments cemented together to form a breccia.

When you're ready, return to the road and turn left. Just before the bridge go through the gate on your right and descend the steps to regain the riverside path. Cross a stile and bear left along the grassy path, still following the Eden upstream but ignoring the very faint path along the riverbank itself. You soon join a fence on your left, and then cross another stile.

After crossing two stiles in quick succession, turn left. When the fence kinks left, keep walking in the same direction and you will eventually cross another two stiles. Head straight across this rough pasture and through a gate.

Cross the track and go through the gate opposite. Bear half-left, passing to the right of a large tree and then go through a gate in a wall. Continuing in the same direction with Wharton Hall below, go through another gate to reach a track, along which you turn left. As you reach a junction at the farm buildings, turn right.

Having crossed a cattle grid, turn left through a large gate. Follow the line of the fence on your left and go through another gate. You now cross two narrower enclosures. After the second one, swing right along a faint trail, which passes to the right of a small rise and then makes for **Lammerside Castle** (see Walk 2 for details). The route heads to the left of the ruins and then through a gate.

Turn left immediately, going through another gate to pick up a rough track beside the river that skirts the base of **Birkett Common**. As the track approaches the farm at **Dalefoot**, on the other side of the river, it swings sharp right, heading upstream, and later passes a lime kiln.

You will see a lot of **lime kilns** throughout the Eden Valley. Limestone was once burned with locally extracted coal or wood, or locally produced charcoal, to produce lime for the fields. It is used to counteract excessive acidity in the soil and enables crops to be grown on marginal land. The lime would also have been used to make mortar for building and whitewash for painting walls.

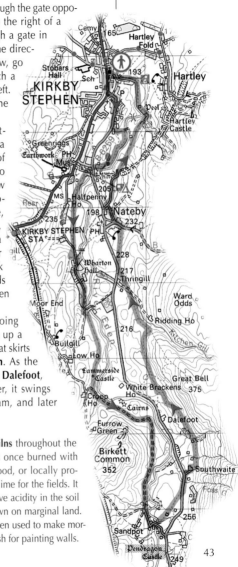

43

Pendragon Castle is closely associated with the legend of King Arthur

At the road turn left. Just after crossing the River Eden, you will see your path signposted to the left, but continue along the road for now to visit **Pendragon Castle**. The castle is on private land, but it can be accessed through a gate on your right at the road junction.

> **Pendragon Castle**, once three storeys high, was built in about 1160 and later came into the possession of the Clifford family. Local legend has it that Uther Pendragon, the father of King Arthur, originally founded the castle. He and a hundred of his men are said to have been killed here when Saxons poisoned the well.

Having explored the ruins, return to the bridge and turn right, aiming to the left of the small building ahead. Go through a gate in the wall and then cross to a short section of wall in the fence ahead. Cross the stile and then continue through the pretty meadow in roughly the same direction.

Turn left at the road, and after about 150m turn right along a farm lane. Having passed a building on your left, swing left and go through the right-hand of the two gates ahead. Turn right, heading gently uphill and through the gate at the top.

Turn left, quickly crossing a small gully, and then head north. About 80m to the right of a tiny building, cross a gill followed by a stile in a wall. Now aim for the building at **Carr House** (named on the Explorer map), the roof of which is visible to the north. Just before dropping towards it, go through the gate on your right and turn left towards another gate providing access to woodland. Keep close to the fence on your left at first. After fording a small beck, the path becomes more obvious. Just before a large gate, bear right to cross a stile in a wall.

A clear path through the bracken keeps close to the wall. Bear right at a waymarker and then right again along a grassy track. Bear left at a fork. Close to the ruined buildings at **Ridding House**, cross a stile next to a gate on your left and then follow Thringill Beck downstream.

Having gone through a gate, continue with the beck on your right until you reach a bridge. Cross this and head towards a large metal gate. Once through, walk with the wall on your left, through another gate in the field corner and then alongside the wall on your right. After a short while, the path swings left across the field to a gate on to the road.

Turn right along the road and and, almost immediately, turn right into the layby. Go through the gated stile on the right and walk with the fence/wall on your left. Having gone through a small gate, bear left to go through a second one. Now walk between two rows of trees to access a shady lane.

Turn left at the road, into **Nateby**, and then right down a narrow lane. Cross any one of the small bridges on your right and then continue with the stream on your left. Turn right along a track between two walls. When this ends, bear right. This lane, making up part of the Poetry Path that you encountered earlier, crosses a bridge over the disused railway, now a permissive bridleway.

Keep right at a fork. The track enters woodland and drops to a bridge. Once over this, make your way over to the River Eden, eventually joining a path coming in from the right. Continue along the river to reach Frank's Bridge on the edge of Kirkby Stephen. Cross this and bear right, between the buildings. Turn right at the top of the steps and then continue straight ahead to return to the church.

> The attractive red sandstone parish church, known locally as the **Cathedral of the Dales**, is well worth a visit. The earliest stone church on the site, part of which can still be seen, dates from the late 12th century. Among the interesting relics inside is the eighth century Loki Stone, one of only two such stones in Europe representing the Norse god.

WALK 4
Kirkby Stephen to Appleby

Distance	15 miles (24.2km)
Total ascent	509m (1670ft)
Start	Kirkby Stephen railway station (NY 761 067)
Finish	Appleby-in-Westmorland railway station (NY 686 206)
Terrain	Limestone grassland, riverside meadows, field paths, woodland
Walking time	6½ hrs
Grade	3
Maps	OS Explorer OL19 or OS Landranger 91
Transport	The start and finish are both on the Settle–Carlisle railway
Refreshments	Variety of pubs and cafés in Appleby

This may be a long walk, but it is by no means hard. Another linear route linking stations on the Settle–Carlisle railway, it meanders through pretty countryside in the upper Eden Valley, perfect for a long, hot summer's day. Crossing limestone uplands to the east of Kirkby Stephen, it then descends to beckside meadows as it follows Scandal Beck downstream to Soulby. Farm paths and tracks then lead to Warcop where you pick up the River Eden, the route of which is followed to Appleby.

Leave **Kirkby Stephen station** and head to the main road, along which you turn right. After about 800m, as you reach the Kirkby Stephen town sign, turn left up a track. Beyond the gate at the top, enter a narrow belt of woodland via a ladder stile in the left-hand corner. Walk with a fence on your left. After leaving the trees, continue alongside the fence and cross a stile in a wall. Following pretty much the same line, you soon walk under the railway, passing earthworks along the way, the remains of a long-abandoned settlement.

Continue south-west, soon picking up the line of a wall on your right for a short while, but then swinging left to cross a stile at the other end of the field. Turn left along the road and then right at the T-junction. When this road bends right, go through the gate on the left.

A track gently climbs the open fell, never straying too far from the wall on the right. When

Map continues on page 48

The fortified manor house of Smardale Hall was built in the 15th and 16th centuries on the site of an older building.

you encounter a wall crossing your path, turn right through the gate to continue with the new wall on your left. Beyond the next gate, aim for the turrets of **Smardale Hall** directly below. ◄

Pick up a rough track beside a wall which drops down to a gate beside a cottage at **Smardale**. Go through to join a lane. Turn left at the T-junction and follow the road round to the left, towards Crosby Garrett. Immediately after the ford take the path on the right. This little-used route passes through pleasant beckside meadows. When you reach a ditch-like track next to a foot-bridge near **Smardale Mill**, continue downstream, crossing the next fence and then going through a gate on the right. The fence on your left is your guide now until you reach a minor road, which you cross to continue beside the beck.

As you approach the next group of buildings, cross a stile on your right and then walk along the edge of the beck. You quickly reach a track coming in from the ford, along which you turn left. Then turn right along a surfaced lane into **Soulby**. Turn right at the road and then left at the crossroads in the village, towards Appleby. When the road bends left a few hundred metres beyond the last buildings, turn right along a gravel track.

When the gravel ends just beyond the buildings at **Sykeside**, bear left towards a metal gate in the field corner

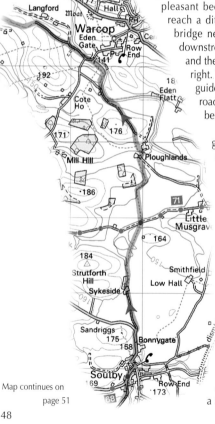

Map continues on page 51

The view across rolling farmland to the North Pennines

to the left of a farm shed. Keep the field boundary on your left and go through a gate. As you enter an area of rough pasture, swing slightly right to cross damp ground to reach a stile. Continuing in the same direction (NNE), cross another stile and continue to reach a minor road.

Turn right and then immediately left, over a small bridge and stile. Keep close to the fence on your right until you reach a gate. Beyond this, continue in the same direction with a tiny beck on your left. Having crossed a stile and bridge, turn right to walk alongside the beck, which soon swings left.

Turn left along a concrete track and follow it round to the right. Just before a gate at **Ploughlands**, cross the stile on the left to follow a tiny beck upstream for a few metres. Then cross the stile on the right and head uphill alongside the hedgerow. Soon after the stile at the top of the first rise, go through a gate to access a rough track with good views towards the North Pennines above Warcop. ▶

After a gate just above the river, keep close to the fence on the right. Having dropped to the water's edge, follow the river to the road on the edge of **Warcop**.

Don't be too alarmed if you hear automatic gunfire or explosions in this area; the Army's Warcop firing ranges are just to the north.

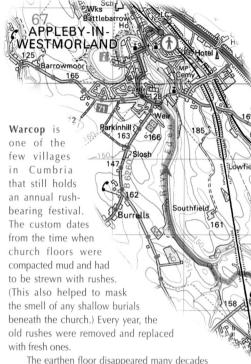

Warcop is one of the few villages in Cumbria that still holds an annual rush-bearing festival. The custom dates from the time when church floors were compacted mud and had to be strewn with rushes. (This also helped to mask the smell of any shallow burials beneath the church.) Every year, the old rushes were removed and replaced with fresh ones.

The earthen floor disappeared many decades ago, but the tradition lives on in Warcop as well as in four other Cumbrian villages: Ambleside, Grasmere, Urswick and Great Musgrave. Warcop's ceremony usually takes place on St Peter's Day, 29 June.

Turn left and in 140m, as the road bends left, take the track on your right. As this begins climbing, turn left along a rough track between hedges. When this bends sharp left, keep straight ahead along a grassy track. After a couple of gates, the track becomes more open as it continues alongside a fence and hedge on your right. The track soon swings right. Leave it when it then swings left by going through the gate on your right. Walk with the field boundary on your right at first, but then go through a small gate to continue with it on your left.

At the bottom of the slope, go through the small gate to the left of the bungalow and then turn right and quickly left along a track towards the farm buildings at **Blacksyke**. As the line of buildings on the right ends, bear half-right through a wooden gate to walk gently uphill between a hedge and some woodland. After a gate, descend gently with a fence on your right, soon picking up a track that takes you to **Little Ormside**.

Follow the road past all the buildings and then, just after crossing a small beck, go through the gate on your left. There is no path on the ground, but you should bear half-right to a stile in a hedge. Continue in the same direction to the next stile after which you swing slightly left of your previous line to go through a large gate. Never too far from the fence on your left, you cross several narrow fields via a succession of stiles to reach a lane.

Turn right along a lane and then, at the T-junction in **Great Ormside**, cross the

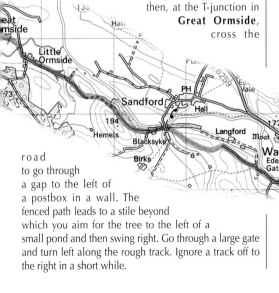

road to go through a gap to the left of a postbox in a wall. The fenced path leads to a stile beyond which you aim for the tree to the left of a small pond and then swing right. Go through a large gate and turn left along the rough track. Ignore a track off to the right in a short while.

After passing under the railway, cross the ladder stile straight ahead and then swing left along a narrow strip of land between two fences. Cross the stile on your right and head downhill, over another stile and down to the footbridge over Jeremy Gill. After climbing the steps on the other side, cross another stile providing access to a clear path through the woods. This eventually swings right, down some steps to the river bank.

You now follow this riverside route practically all the way to Appleby. Sometimes you are in woodland, sometimes in fields, but always following the **River Eden** downstream. As you near the town you will reach a metal gate with a dilapidated stile to the right of it. Ignore this and cross a stile a few feet to the left. A well-trodden path leads to a lane behind **Appleby Castle**. Turn left here and then right at the T-junction.

Follow this road to the castle's front gates, down along Boroughgate into the town and then round to the right. After crossing the River Eden, turn left at the T-junction and then cross the road to access a path heading uphill. At the top turn left and then right, up Clifford Street. **Appleby railway station** is at the top.

Making hay while the sun shines

APPLEBY-IN-WESTMORLAND

Appleby is definitely worth exploring if you have time before your train. It developed as a market town soon after the Norman Conquest, its charter dating back to 1174. The castle (sadly closed to the public) also dates from Norman times, and although much of it was rebuilt in the 17th century, the splendid keep, known as Caesar's Tower, is 12th century.

Like many castles in the area, and other buildings in Appleby, it owes its continuing existence to the efforts of Lady Anne Clifford, a strong-willed and passionate member of the local aristocracy during the 17th century. She was born in Skipton Castle in 1590, the sole heir of the third earl of Cumberland. She failed to inherit her father's Westmorland estates on his death; they eventually passed to her uncle and then her cousin. She fought hard to regain what was rightfully hers and even made a direct, although unsuccessful, appeal to the king. Eventually, her cousin died without a male heir and Lady Anne won back her estates.

On the death of her second husband she moved into Appleby Castle and began a massive project, restoring her castles at Brough, Brougham (see Walk 16) and Pendragon.

Every June the tranquillity of this peaceful town is shattered as thousands of Romany families, some in colourful, horse-drawn caravans, arrive for the centuries-old horse fair, the largest of its kind in the world.

St Anne's Hospital in Appleby, a group of almshouses founded by Lady Anne Clifford for poor widows in the mid-17th century

WALK 5

Smardale Gill

Distance	8½ miles (13.7km)
Total ascent	378m (1240ft)
Start/finish	The Crosby Garrett bridleway sign on the open fell road between Newbiggin-on-Lune and Great Asby (NY 693 062), 1 mile north of the A685 at Newbiggin-on-Lune. Park on the grass verge nearby.
Terrain	Open moorland and a disused railway
Walking time	4½ hrs
Grade	2–3
Maps	OS Explorer OL19 or OS Landranger 91
Transport	Crosby Garrett is served by bus 571
Refreshments	Black Swan in nearby Ravenstonedale

This is a walk of many parts. It starts with an easy stroll on the edge of open moorland along Wainwright's Coast to Coast route and then makes use of an interesting footpath following the line of a disused railway. There are a number of fascinating features along this first half of the walk, including a prehistoric settlement, a National Nature Reserve and the impressive Smardale Gill Viaduct. After a short section of road walking, the second part of the walk crosses wind-swept Crosby Garrett Fell.

From the Crosby Garrett bridleway sign head towards Crosby Garrett with the drystone wall on your right. The faint grassy path soon becomes more track-like. The walking is pure joy after the track goes through a gate in a wall running perpendicular to the one you are following. There is no route-finding to worry about; simply keep close to the wall on your right at every fork. As you stride out easily on the short turf you can relax and enjoy the lovely views: to the south-east are Wild Boar Fell and Mallerstang; to the south and south-west, the horizon is dominated by the rounded tops of the Howgills.

▶ At the green sign to **Bents Farm**, keep straight ahead. Where the wall bends left and begins heading uphill, go through the gate and follow a faint path close to the wall on your right. About 275m beyond the gate, cross the stile in the wall and turn left to continue with the wall now on your left.

Bents Farm is home to a camping barn popular with Coast to Coast walkers.

The area to your right contains the village known as **Severals**, one of the most extensive prehistoric settlements found in Britain. The complex of huts, dykes, paths and enclosures covers about three acres but, when combined with two other settlements just to the north, extends to about a hundred acres.

Follow the path signs when you reach a ruined cottage, which indicate that you must turn right at the building and then left through a gate and over the old railway bridge. Immediately after the bridge, turn right and cross the wooden stile on your right to gain the disused Tebay–Darlington line. Turn right along the railway, immediately passing under the bridge you just crossed.

This section of the **South Durham and Lancashire Union Railway**, also known as the Stainmore Railway,

Crosby Garrett

195

209

Tunnel

Ford

Hall

Smardale

Nettle Hill
382

Crosby Garrett Fell

Demesne Wood

365

Great Ewe Fell

Cairn

Settlements

Settlement

304

Smardale Gill
National Nature Reserve

Begin Hill

Brackenber

Settlement

Bents Fm

272

Brownber

Earthwork

221

Smardale Br

55

Hill

A lime kiln beside the old Tebay–Darlington railway

opened in 1861, and the kilns that you pass in a short while supplied lime to the steelworks in both Darlington and Barrow. The primary purpose of the railway was to take coke from County Durham to the iron and steel furnaces of Barrow and west Cumbria. When the Barrow steelworks closed, the line was axed soon after in 1962.

Before long the disused railway crosses the massive **Smardale Gill Viaduct**, crossing Scandal Beck far below, and then enters woodland. ◀

The 14-arch Smardale Gill Viaduct is 90ft tall and is a listed building. For a better sense of its scale, walk along the path to the right immediately after crossing it.

The woods here are part of **Smardale Gill National Nature Reserve**, which consists mostly of limestone grassland. It is home to rare plants including several types of orchid and the nationally rare bird's-foot sedge. Two important butterfly species are also found here: the northern brown argus and the Scotch argus. It is one of only two sites in England where a population of the latter may be found.

The railway path ends near **Smardale Hall**. When you reach a rough lane opposite a small parking area turn left and then left again. Follow this quiet country lane for about 1.7km, crossing **Scandal Beck** via a ford/footbridge on the way. When you reach **Crosby Garrett**, cross the small stream in the village and turn left. Walk under the viaduct and continue straight ahead, crossing a cattle grid

and then passing a white cottage on the moorland edge on your right.

Smardale Gill Viaduct

Immediately after the cottage, turn right and head uphill, passing to the left of a small, fenced enclosure to join a stony/grassy track heading south-west up on to the fell. About 275m beyond the cottage the track forks; bear right to keep close to the shallow gully on the right. When the limestone outcrop in the gully disappears, the path becomes much fainter. Keep heading uphill in the same direction across tussocky ground. At the top of the climb, when you can finally see across to the Lake District in the distance, the path becomes a little more obvious as it makes a distinct swing left across Crosby Garrett Fell. Join another, clearer bridleway coming in from the right at a waymarker. With the Howgills directly ahead, begin a gentle descent.

After going through a gate in a fence, ignore a narrower trail off to the right. The track eventually descends more steeply and you will see **Bents Farm** ahead. Be careful not to be distracted by the many paths heading off in all directions – keep heading for the farmhouse.

When you reach the green 'Bents Farm' sign that you passed early in the walk, turn right and retrace your steps back to the road.

WALK 6
Great Asby Scar

Distance	8½ miles (13.7km)
Total ascent	317m (1040ft)
Start/finish	Small layby with a bench and litter-bin on the B6261, 400m east of Orton (NY 629 080)
Terrain	Good bridleways on open limestone moorland and tracks
Walking time	4hrs
Grade	2–3
Maps	OS Explorer OL19 or OS Landranger 91
Transport	Nearby Orton is served by bus 106
Refreshments	George Hotel, Orton

This lovely excursion into the fascinating limestone scenery of Great Asby Scar above Orton makes use of pleasant, well signposted bridleways. The relatively gentle climbs are short and well spaced, and the going underfoot is generally good. With little need to worry about rocky or muddy ground, you can spend more time enjoying this area's unusual geological features and the superb ever-changing views – one minute the Howgills, the next the North Pennines and, finally, the eastern Lake District fells.

From the layby walk eastwards along the minor road towards Raisbeck and Ravenstonedale, occasionally still pronounced 'Rassendul'. After about 1km, having ignored the minor road to Scarside, turn left along a rough track. A fingerpost indicates that this is a public byway. After about 350m turn right over a stile beside a gate.

You are now following part of Wainwright's famous **Coast to Coast long-distance walk**. This 190-mile route, devised by the guidebook writer in 1972, passes through some of England's most beautiful scenery. Starting in St Bees in Cumbria and ending in Robin Hood's Bay in North Yorkshire, it crosses three National Parks: the Lake District, the Yorkshire Dales and the North York Moors.

Heading east in an almost straight line for about 1.5km, walk across several fields with a series of gates/ stiles and occasional waymarkers to guide you. You have the wall on your right at first but then pass through a gate/ stile to continue with it on your left. Then, just after an old barn, you lose the line of the wall, but the route remains obvious as it crosses stiles and passes through gates. The route ahead is less clear as you enter the final field; you should now aim for the building at **Acres** straight ahead. When you reach the minor road in front of this farmhouse turn left. As the road bends to the right near the next set of dwellings at **Sunbiggin**, turn left up a track.

This climbs easily between drystone walls and then passes to the left of a farm build- ing. Go through the 'pallet' gate straight ahead and then a

The long line of the North Pennines stretches into the distance as you reach the highest point on the walk

large wooden gate with a yellow waymarker beside it. Continuing in the same direction cross several fields via a series of clearly waymarked gates, climbing gently all the while.

Having passed through a small gate at the top of a slightly steeper climb, you leave the enclosures behind and find yourself on open limestone country. Head northeast on a narrow grassy path through the rock outcrops, being careful not to be tempted by quad bike tracks off to the right. The highest point on the walk comes just after a pole with a yellow marker on it.

Soon after the pole, cross a wider track and keep straight on towards the small gate. Go through and keep straight ahead on a faint path with a fence to your right. Go through the next gate and then, a few metres later, go through a gate on your right. Turn left along the grassy track for a just a few metres, soon leaving it by bearing left at a faint fork to keep close to the fence on the left. When you reach a drystone wall, go through the gate and follow the indistinct path, keeping close to the wall on your right. Eventually you reach a vehicle track where you turn left, towards Sayle Lane, and then left again at the road.

Walk along the asphalt for about 400m and then, at a right-hand bend, turn left up a wide track, known as Copper Mine Lane. When this ends at a gate, go through and keep straight ahead with a wall on your left. Go through the next gate and when the path forks in a few metres, bear right, up the hill towards a small gate.

Go through the gate to gain access to **Great Asby Scar National Nature Reserve**. Follow the narrow but clear path south-west, skirting the edge of the limestone pavement at first but then climbing slightly to walk straight through the middle of this fascinating scenery.

Grazing has been stopped on **Great Asby Scar NNR** to allow dwarf trees and deep heather to grow. The area is home to a number of rare plants, including Solomon's seal, rigid buckler fern and both black and green spleenwort ferns, although you may have to peer deep into the grikes to see them.

Crossing Great Asby Scar

Turn left at a T-junction with a wider path, and climb easily to a gate at the south-west edge of the reserve. Once through the gate, follow the clear path on close-cropped grass. In a short while the distant views change yet again, and it is the eastern Lake District fells that now demand attention.

About 500m beyond the nature reserve, turn left at a fingerpost at the end of the escarpment, through the gate. A grassy path contours the hillside, becoming more track-like as it descends. When the track goes through a gate and passes a lime kiln, you will be able to see (but sadly not visit) a large **stone circle** in a field ahead and slightly off to the left. Turn right when you reach the road and retrace your steps to the parking area.

WALK 7
Crosby Ravensworth Fell

Distance	6½ miles (10.5km)
Total ascent	253m (830ft)
Start/finish	Crosby Ravensworth village hall (NY 620 147)
Terrain	Farm paths and grassy tracks on open heather moorland
Walking time	3½ hrs
Grade	2–3
Maps	OS Explorer OL19 or OS Landranger 91
Transport	Crosby Ravensworth is served by bus 562
Refreshments	Butcher's Arms in Crosby Ravensworth

This beautiful expanse of low limestone moorland is steeped in history: from ancient pre-Roman settlements to Charles I's journey south to his final, unsuccessful battle of the Civil War. The best time to visit is the late summer when the sweet smell of flowering heather fills the air and the ground is a carpet of purple.

With your back to **Crosby Ravensworth** village hall, turn right along the road and then go through a metal gate on the right, signposted Holme Bridge. Once through the next gate, straight in front of you, walk beside the fence on your right. Go through the gate at the end of this track and then climb the ladder stile on your right. Turn left to reach the pretty **Lyvennet Beck** and follow it upstream.

The name '**Lyvennet**' is closely associated with the post-Roman Celtic kingdom of Rheged, which covered much of modern-day Cumbria. It is thought that Urien, who had a number of victories over Anglian chieftains in the second half of the sixth century, ruled from 'Llwyfenydd'. Urien was a descendant of Coel Han, or 'Old King Cole'. His son was Uwain, one of the kingdom's greatest heroes who inspired his men to fight rather than give tribute to the English.

The stories of Rheged are steeped in myth and legend, so it is hard to talk with any certainty about 'historical facts'. Some, for instance, claim that Llwyfenydd was in Wales and the Lyvennet was merely named after it; others will tell you that Llwyfenydd and Lyvennet are, in fact, the same place.

You soon cross a wooden step stile, beyond which keep close to the fence on the left. Having crossed a stile in this fence, bear right to head towards the road bridge. Turn left at the road. Immediately after crossing the bridge, go through the gap on your right and then cross the stile in the fence. Walk with the fence on your right.

Keeping close to the field boundary on your right, cross the next wall via a stone stile to the right of a metal gate. Once over the next stile you lose the guiding fence/wall on your right, so head straight across to the wall on the opposite side of the enclosure and cross the well-camouflaged stone stile to the left of the gate.

The lines of stones and remains of hut circles to the left belong to Burwens, a settlement thought to have been inhabited by ancient Britons long before the Romans arrived.

Continuing southwards, head gently uphill to the immediate left of some trees. Maintain the same direction to walk with a fence on your right. Go through the next metal gate on the right to head downhill on a track. Just beyond the gate in the bottom of the valley, turn left at a T-junction to head gently uphill. ◄

Looking back along the track leading to Crosby Lodge, with Cross Fell in the background

Soon after passing a solitary barn to the right of the track, cross the stile in the wall on the right. Bear left, heading for a gap in a wall to the right of the buildings at **Crosby Lodge**. Go through the gate on the right and then, having dropped away from the wall, turn left. You quickly go through a gate next to a solitary tree.

Keep close to the wall on the left. On the other side of the field, follow the vehicle track through the gate and stick with it until you reach a fork, where you bear left. Once through the next gate you lose the vehicle track, so head southwards straight across the field. As you approach a wall on the other side, bear half-right to head down to a gate where a fence meets the wall. Go through and immediately cross the wall via a stile on the left. ▶

The open fell here is dotted with burial cairns, stone circles and the remains of ancient settlements.

Turn right to walk alongside the wall on **Crosby Ravensworth Fell**. The path soon drops steeply into a dry valley, typical of limestone country. Once you've climbed out the other side, keep close to the fence/wall on your right. The path dips again to cross a tiny beck and then continues to follow the wall. Having followed the wall as it kinks its way up the fell, the clear grassy swathe you are walking on comes away from it slightly.

As you make your way towards the slope leading on to higher ground, the path splits; follow either branch, they soon meet up again. Having forded the shallow infant Lyvennet at the base of the slope, the path heads uphill, following the line of wooden posts and passing two round boulders, erratics deposited here by a glacier during the last Ice Age.

Just up the valley from here is the **Black Dub Monument**. Erected in 1843 close to the source of the Lyvennet, it marks the spot where, in August 1651, Charles II and his men stopped for water on their way south from Scotland. Having done a deal with the Scottish Covenanters and been crowned king at Scone, he had been hoping to reassert the rule of the Crown in England. His forces, however, were defeated by Cromwell's more powerful New Model Army at the Battle of Worcester on 3 September.

Pass to the left of a small limestone outcrop to reach a post at the top of the rise and a potentially confusing junction of paths. Bear left here along the wider path, and, almost immediately, bear right when it splits again

Late summer on Crosby Ravensworth Fell

(NNE, soon veering north). Cross straight over another grassy track and head up to the limestone pavement.

◄ Head north-west to a pair of wooden posts, and just beyond them you reach a junction. There are two paths to the right here; take the one that passes to the left of two trees growing out of the limestone pavement (NNE). As you draw level with the larger of the two trees, bear left when the track splits to maintain the same direction. After fording a small beck, head straight up the grassy slope on the other side. This track follows almost the same line as Wicker Street, the Roman road linking the fort at Low Borrow Bridge on the Lune with either Brougham or Kirkby Thore.

Nearing the top of the small rise, turn right along another wide, grassy track, heading north-east. As you stride out across the open moorland, you gradually find yourself being funnelled into an ever narrowing strip of access land between two drystone walls; ignore any paths to the right and keep closer to the wall on the left. Eventually, the grassy path becomes more solid underfoot and then joins a track coming in from the right. On reaching the road, turn left and walk back to the village hall at **Crosby Ravensworth**.

At 357m (1171ft) this is the highest point on the walk; it has superb, all-round views of the Pennines, the Howgills and, ahead, the eastern Lake District fells.

WALK 8
Maulds Meaburn and the Lyvennet Valley

Distance	5 miles (8.2km)
Total ascent	183m (600ft)
Start/finish	Phone box in Maulds Meaburn, close to the more southerly of the village's two road bridges over the Lyvennet (NY 625 162)
Terrain	Field and meadow paths
Walking time	2½ hrs
Grade	2
Maps	OS Explorer OL19 or OS Landranger 91
Transport	Maulds Meaburn is served by bus 562
Refreshments	Butcher's Arms in Crosby Ravensworth

This walk presents an opportunity to visit two lovely villages in the pretty Lyvennet valley. Starting from the tranquil Maulds Meaburn, strung out along an open green where sheep graze, it then heads upstream to Crosby Ravensworth. Passing the ruins of a 14th-century fortified house along the way, it crosses meadows and rolling farmland, always with superb views of the North Pennines.

From the phone box in **Maulds Meaburn**, walk south along the road, quickly crossing the bridge over the Lyvennet signposted Appleby. Follow the main road round to the right and then turn right at the second finger-post, along a surfaced lane. Go through the small gate to the left of the entrance to **Flass House**. ▶

Pass under a bridge to enter a field, which you cross diagonally. A squeeze stile leads to a riverside path which takes you all the way to **Crosby Ravensworth**. As you draw level with the primary school on the other side of the beck, go through an old metal gate and cross the grass to reach the road. Cross the bridge on your right and turn left along the road. Soon, pick up a footpath on

Flass House is a rather grand Palladian-style mansion dating from the mid-19th century.

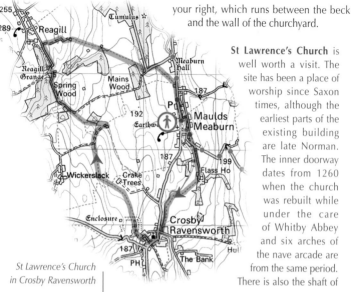

your right, which runs between the beck and the wall of the churchyard.

St Lawrence's Church is well worth a visit. The site has been a place of worship since Saxon times, although the earliest parts of the existing building are late Norman. The inner doorway dates from 1260 when the church was rebuilt while under the care of Whitby Abbey and six arches of the nave arcade are from the same period. There is also the shaft of

St Lawrence's Church in Crosby Ravensworth

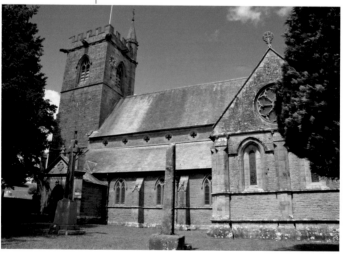

a medieval stone cross in the churchyard, although the cross itself was lost many centuries ago.

About 150m beyond the church there is a ford. Turn right here, along a track heading straight between the farm buildings. When you clear the farmyard turn left along a rough track, which quickly swings right to climb gently. There is a sense of the track swinging left as it reaches the top of the rise. At this point, go through the gate straight ahead and then cut diagonally across the field to its far left-hand corner.

Cross three stiles in quick succession and then bear half-left through the next field. Aim for a wooden farm gate about 100m to the left of the buildings at **Crake Trees**. Bear half-right through this narrow enclosure to reach a squeeze stile in the wall. Once over the small bridge on the other side, head to the left of the ruins and the large tree next to them.

In the spring and early summer there is a good chance of seeing curlews and lapwings in these fields.

The ruins at **Crake Trees** are all that remain of a 14th-century fortified tower house, probably built for the Lancaster family of Sockbridge Hall near Penrith. Two storeys high, it would have had a banqueting hall and chapel. The original timber-framed great hall was demolished in the late 16th century, and the stone walls that can be seen today date from the late 16th or early 17th centuries.

After a squeeze stile, walk uphill beside the fence. The next stile, partly hidden by a hawthorn bush, is a little difficult to spot, but once you are over it turn right to walk alongside the wall. Continue in the same direction through the next two fields, walking parallel with a fence over to your left in the first one and then keeping close to the boundary on your right in the second.

On reaching a junction of routes after the next stile, take the path going through the farm gate straight ahead. Head in the general direction of Cross Fell in the distance at first, then veer away from the beck on your left to drop towards an unusual barn. At the waymarker to the left of the building, turn sharp left, aiming for the top end of a small area of trees where you will find a bridge over the beck that you were following when you first entered this field.

Go through a small gate and keep close to the field boundary on your right. Continue through another two gates and then cross a field, heading up a slope at first and then aiming to the right of the shed. You soon pick up a track that passes the shed, runs alongside Spring Wood and then leads up through the farmyard at **Reagill Grange**. Pass the 18th-century house on your right and then join a surfaced lane heading gently uphill.

About 400m beyond the grange, turn right along a rough track. With the Pennines directly ahead, follow the track to Beechtree Farm. Pass to the left of the building and then swing right, still on the track, through an orchard. As the track begins to swing right, leave it by going through the gate straight ahead.

Look to the left of the woods straight ahead and you will see a squat building. Your next stile lies between that building and the woods. There is a vague path on the ground leading to it which goes straight down the slope and then swings left between the saplings. Once over the stile, keep close to the woods on the right and then, in about 200m, go through a farm gate. The path now swings away from the woods, making for a stile in a fence to the south-east. Beyond this head slightly right across the huge field to reach a footbridge close to three tall pine trees. Cross the stile at the top of the embankment and then bear half-right through this narrow belt of young trees.

Turn right along the road and, immediately after Howebeck Bridge, cross the stile on the right. Head south-east across the field. ◄ You will see **Meaburn Hall** over the wall on your left and, about 275m beyond this, go through a stile in said wall. Bear half-right to drop to your final stile of the day, just to the left of a small cottage. Turn right along the road to return to **Maulds Meaburn**. (The word 'Meaburn' is thought to derive from the Anglo-Saxon *Meadburn*, meaning 'meadow by the stream'.)

Built in 1610, Meaburn Hall was an early seat of the Lowther family, still one of the biggest landowners in the whole of Cumbria.

Pretty Maulds Meaburn straddles the Lyvennet

WALK 9

Rutter Force

Distance	5 miles (8.1km)
Total ascent	183m (600ft)
Start/finish	The lane leading to Oakbeck and Drybeck in Hoff, about 2 miles south-west of Appleby, opposite the bus stop (NY 675 175). There is off-road parking for a few cars at the beginning of this lane.
Terrain	Farm paths and tracks
Walking time	2½ hours
Grade	1–2
Maps	OS Explorer OL19 or OS Landranger 91
Transport	Hoff is served by bus 561
Refreshments	Variety of pubs and cafés in nearby Appleby

Whatever time of year you visit, Rutter Force is always an interesting spot: dramatic in winter, when river levels are high and a powerful torrent comes raging down the cliff; idyllic in summer when a fine veil of water shrouds part of the back wall and then gently flows past the picturesque red sandstone corn mill. This walk approaches the waterfall via a lovely beckside path that starts near the hamlet of Hoff. It then crosses farmland, often on unmarked paths, and passes through woods that are home to hundreds of pheasants.

From **Hoff**, walk along the lane initially heading south-east, towards Oakbeck and Drybeck, for about 300m and then turn left along a rough track, which is not signposted. When you reach **Hoff Beck** go through a gate. Keep close to the water's edge and cross the footbridge. Turn right to follow the beck upstream for about 1km.

Having crossed several stiles along the way and passed one vehicle-wide bridge, you need to re-cross the beck via a wooden, railed footbridge with waymarkers on it. Now turn left to continue upstream along the other side of the beck. After the next stile, close to an unusually large boulder in the middle of the beck, follow a trail slightly back from the water's edge which leads to a surfaced lane.

The best view is from the footbridge next to the ford.

The walk route crosses straight over, but to see **Rutter Force** and the mill, turn left. ◄

Rutter Mill, which now provides holiday accommodation, has served many purposes during its long lifetime. It has been a corn mill, a bobbin mill and a timber mill. From 1928 until 1951 it was even used to generate

electricity – albeit an unreliable supply – for homes in and around Great Asby.

Rutter Force and the mill

Back on track again, having crossed the lane just up from the mill and cottages, take the footpath opposite, which quickly goes through a small gate. Ignore a flight of steps up to the right and pass round the back of the buildings. After a stile, follow the trail through the beck-side vegetation. This brings you to a gate, beyond which you continue upstream.

As the flat area between the water on your left and the trees on your right widens, keep close to the trees. Cross a stile in a fence and then, keeping close to the water, cross a stile in a wall to the left of a large gate. The beckside route passes a vehicle-wide bridge and reaches a waymarked fork close to a footbridge. Keep straight on, ignoring the bridge. The route comes away from the beck slightly, passing to the left of old quarry workings. Just beyond this line of exposed rock, go through a gate and swing right, along a rough track through woodland.

Having climbed gently for about 200m, watch for a gate in the wall on the left. Cross the stile next to it and bear half-right to cut diagonally across a series of fields. There are no paths on the ground and no obvious landmarks to guide you, but you need to head NNW at first, eventually veering north-west towards the farm buildings at **Haybanks**.

As you emerge on a rough lane beside the farm, turn left and then left again at the road. Having passed the 17th-century **Drybeck Hall**, turn right at the T-junction in **Drybeck** and then, almost immediately, go through the large wooden gate on your right. Head uphill beside the wall. At the top of the climb go through the gate and continue in the same direction, with the field boundary on your left.

Drop down to an area of woodland, **Hoff Lunn**, and enter over a stile; turn left immediately to cross a bridge. As indicated by a waymarker, the path swings right, down a steep slope and crosses the beck at the bottom via a small bridge. Climb straight up the embankment and then walk between the trees on your left and a fenced area on

The walk back along the road provides good views across rolling farmland to the Pennines beyond

your right. When you reach a track continue along this in the same direction as before. ▸

After a gate, drop towards Hofflunn Farm and then follow the track as it swings left. Cross the stile beside the next gate to re-enter the woods. This rough track leads all the way to the road, but be careful not to lose sight of it. A little way into the woods it becomes very indistinct, so make sure you swing right here to cross a mossy, well-camouflaged bridge beyond which you begin to climb between tall conifers. Turn right along the road; it is now just under 2km back to **Hoff**.

This is a pheasant breeding area, with dozens of young birds running around during the summer.

WALK 10
River Lyvennet at King's Meaburn

Distance	6¼ miles (10km)
Total ascent	204m (670ft)
Start/finish	White Horse Inn, King's Meaburn (NY 620 212)
Terrain	Field and riverside paths, quiet lanes and tracks
Walking time	3hrs
Grade	2
Maps	OS Explorer OL19 or OS Landranger 91
Transport	King's Meaburn is served by bus 562
Refreshments	White Horse Inn, King's Meaburn

This gentle stroll follows the River Lyvennet as it meanders its way through woods and meadows close to King's Meaburn. The route then heads away from the water, ambling along quiet country lanes, tracks and bridleways through pleasant, gently rolling countryside with good views of both the Pennines and the Lake District fells.

With your back to the pub, turn left along the road out of **King's Meaburn**. After passing the national speed limit sign, go through a gap in the wall on the left. With no obvious path on the ground, cut diagonally across the

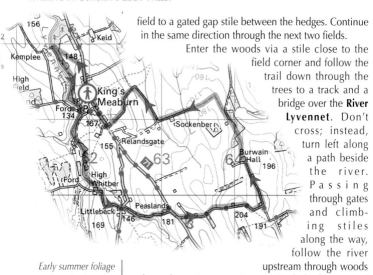

field to a gated gap stile between the hedges. Continue in the same direction through the next two fields.

Enter the woods via a stile close to the field corner and follow the trail down through the trees to a track and a bridge over the **River Lyvennet**. Don't cross; instead, turn left along a path beside the river. Passing through gates and climbing stiles along the way, follow the river upstream through woods and meadows. As you enter a particularly dark area of

Early summer foliage on the Lyvennet

King's Meaburn Mill

woodland, bear right at a split in the path, keeping close to the water's edge. ▶

Eventually, you pass a beautifully placed riverside cottage to reach a road leading to a ford. To pick up the continuation of the riverside path, turn right along this road and then immediately left. A stile provides access to a woodland trail continuing with the river on your right.

When you reach the bridge leading to King's Meaburn Mill, do not cross it; instead, cross the rough track and climb the partly hidden stile. The path can be a bit tricky after the next stile where tree roots and slippery rocks have become exposed. Beyond this, though, you are on the riverbank again with a lovely view back towards the old mill.

After the next stile, the path passes very close to the river's edge. This short section might present difficulties when water levels are particularly high. One more stile and the path keeps close to the woods on your left, beginning to head away from the water's edge. As the fence comes to an end, swing slightly left and then aim for a gate in the hedge straight ahead.

Jackdaws' Scar, partly hidden by the trees up to your left, is unusual in that it has a layer of exposed limestone on top of a layer of sandstone.

Beyond this, cross the field to a small footbridge. Now swing half-left along a trail, passing about 200m to the left of the farmhouse at **High Whitber**. Once over a stile beside a gate, turn left along the lane. Turn left at the minor road and then immediately right along a rough track.

Turn right at the T-junction and take the next road on your left towards Colby and Appleby. Savouring the occasional tantalising glimpse of the North Pennines

Looking across to the eastern Lake District fells from Sockenber

through gaps in the high hedges as you go, walk along this quiet lane for about 1km. When the road bends sharp right, turn left along a wide track beside a house with what must undoubtedly be distracting but enviable views.

The track ends at **Burwain Hall**. Go through the double gate to the right of the old house and walk with the fence on your left. On entering the woods, continue in the same direction along a grassy, sometimes muddy path. Soon after crossing a tiny beck, pick up a rough track. After a gate, leave the track by going through another gate straight ahead to access a bridleway between two fences. It may at first look rather overgrown, but the path is easy to follow.

Eventually emerging from the undergrowth, walk down the track immediately ahead. After passing the farm at **Sockenber**, descend towards a caravan park. Just in front of the site entrance, turn right along a rough track. After 400m, it is possible to cut a corner by crossing the wall on your left at a fingerpost, aiming for the footbridge straight ahead and then walking up the field to a stile in the hedges. However, the track normally makes for pleasant easy walking, so there's no need for the short-cut unless the next muddy section is a problem.

Follow the track round to the left and climb to a T-junction. Turn right and follow the road through the village and back to the pub in **King's Meaburn**.

Both **King's Meaburn** and **Maulds Meaburn** were once in the barony of the 12th-century knight Sir Hugh de Morville, the Lord of Westmorland. He forfeited the land after he and three other knights killed Thomas à Becket, the Archbishop of Canterbury, in 1170. The northern part of the manor reverted to the Crown, and has since been known as King's Meaburn, while the southern part went to Morville's sister Maud, hence Maulds Meaburn.

WALK 11

River Lowther at Bampton Grange

Distance	5 miles (8km)
Total ascent	82m (270ft)
Start/finish	St Patrick's Church, Bampton Grange (NY 521 180)
Terrain	Quiet lanes, riverside paths and farmland
Walking time	2hrs
Grade	1
Maps	OS Explorer OL5 or OS Landranger 90
Transport	Bampton Grange is served by bus 111
Refreshments	Crown and Mitre, Bampton Grange

The River Lowther flows through gently rolling countryside close to the base of the Lake District's far eastern fells. This walk starts in the quiet, slightly off-the-beaten-track village of Bampton Grange and uses farm paths, riverside trails and some country lanes to explore this peaceful corner of the National Park. Walk the route at dawn or dusk and there's a chance of seeing deer, badgers or even otters.

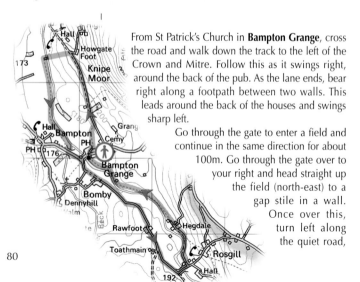

From St Patrick's Church in **Bampton Grange**, cross the road and walk down the track to the left of the Crown and Mitre. Follow this as it swings right, around the back of the pub. As the lane ends, bear right along a footpath between two walls. This leads around the back of the houses and swings sharp left.

Go through the gate to enter a field and continue in the same direction for about 100m. Go through the gate over to your right and head straight up the field (north-east) to a gap stile in a wall. Once over this, turn left along the quiet road,

soon crossing a cattle grid. Continue along the open road as it crosses **Knipe Moor**.

The River Lowther runs close to the base of the Lake District's far eastern fells

As you draw level with a farm track heading up to the right, turn left just in front of the rectangular stone construction beside the road. Cross the bridge over the River Lowther and turn left, through a small gate, to gain a lovely riverside path.

OTTERS IN THE EDEN VALLEY

There are otters throughout the Eden catchment, and several have been seen along the River Lowther. Having been driven to the brink of extinction during the second half of the 20th century, these elusive creatures are making a dramatic comeback on Cumbria's rivers.

Otter numbers began to decline seriously in the 1950s. Although factors such as habitat loss, changes to land management, hunting and road deaths were partly to blame, the main cause seems to have been the growing use of pesticides such as dieldrin. This poison, used as a seed dressing and in sheep-dip, found its way into watercourses and fish stock. The reproductive ability of otters, feeding on the contaminated fish, was severely impaired. Only as dieldrin was slowly withdrawn from use, and then banned entirely in 1989, did otter numbers begin to recover. ▶

You need to be both quiet and patient if you want to see an otter; they are notoriously difficult to spot. Keep your eyes peeled for their prints in the soft mud on the river bank. Otters have five webbed toes, although it is common for only four to show up in prints; the rear paw print tends to be longer. Also watch for holes in the bank, especially near trees with large root systems, or for piles of sticks and brambles at the edge of the water; these could indicate an entrance to a holt. Otters tend not to dig their own homes, they will use natural holes or even old rabbit burrows.

Solitary male otters and family groups have their own territories, which they mark by leaving smelly droppings, or spraints, in prominent locations such as on large boulders or at the base of tree trunks. Spraints tend to be black and tarry, containing a lot of fish bones, but the only sure-fire way of recognising an otter spraint is to sniff it; its smell has been variously described as fishy or like freshly-mown hay, jasmine tea or lavender.

After following the river upstream for about 800m keep your eyes peeled for a ladder stile close to the river. You will have been walking on a raised embankment for quite some time, and the ladder stile is a few metres to the left of it, so it is easy to miss it. Having crossed the stile, keep close to the river bank until you reach the road. Now turn left, crossing the Lowther.

On reaching the edge of **Bampton Grange**, turn right along the minor road, towards Haweswater and Mardale. When the road forks shortly, bear left towards Swindale and Rosgill. Pass **Bomby** and the farmhouse at **Rawfoot**, and ignore the road up to Swindale on your right. Keep to the Rosgill road, following it as it bends left to cross the River Lowther. Just as the road begins to climb, turn left along a narrow lane.

As you approach the farmhouse at **Hegdale**, bear left to walk along a rough track between two drystone walls. Pass a barn on your left and go through a gate, keeping close to the wall on the right. After the next gate/stile the path edges closer to the river. Cross a plank bridge, followed by another gate/stile, and continue downstream.

Bampton Grange

Cross a stone stile in the wall at the far end of this meadow, followed shortly by a gated squeeze stile leading into another field. Make directly for the church in **Bampton Grange**, and go through a small gate and then a kissing-gate to enter the churchyard. Pass around the back of the church to leave via a small gate opposite the pub.

St Patrick's Church was built in the 18th century, but the first mention of a church on this site occurs as early as 1170 when the Premonstratensian canons (or 'white canons' after the colour of their habits) of nearby Shap Abbey held services here. The riverside path from Rosgill forms part of the route that the canons would have taken from Shap.

The vicarage, opposite the church, is home to the Tinklar Library, which contains an important collection of Latin books.

WALK 12

Lowther Park

Distance	7¼ miles (11.8km)
Total ascent	242m (795ft)
Start/finish	Community centre car park in Askham (NY 512 238)
Terrain	Roads, tracks, fields and woodland paths
Walking time	3hrs
Grade	1–2
Maps	OS Explorer OL5 or OS Landranger 90
Transport	Askham is served by bus 111; Clifton is served by bus 106
Refreshments	The Queen's Head, Askham; café at the Askham Stores; George and Dragon, Clifton

Crossing the heart of Lowther country on the edge of the Lake District National Park, this easy walk has plenty of historical and wildlife interest. It passes standing stones, a pele tower, Lowther Castle and the site of the last ever battle on English soil. As you go from parkland throuh fields to woods and a riverside path, keep your eyes peeled for deer, red squirrels, herons and buzzards.

Leave the car park in **Askham** and turn left along the road. Ignore the first turning on your left after the Queen's Head, but take the next one, after Askham Stores. The road crosses the River Lowther and, once over the cattle grid, enters **Lowther Park**.

THE LOWTHER FAMILY

For centuries this area has been associated with the Lowther family, the largest private landowners in Cumbria. One of the oldest families in England, their arms are documented as far back as the late 12th century. Much of the family's modern wealth came from the coal fields of west Cumbria, and they are often credited with bringing the Industrial Revolution to Cumberland many years before it reached other north-western counties.

Probably the most famous of the Lowthers was the fifth Earl of Lonsdale, Hugh Cecil Lowther (1857–1944), who was passionate about sport. A celebrated horseman and yachtsman, he was also well-known in boxing circles where he initiated the presentation of the celebrated Lonsdale Belt to British champions. Because of his liking for yellow livery on his cars, horse boxes and coachmen, Hugh Lowther was dubbed the 'Yellow Earl', and his Lonsdale yellow was adopted by the Automobile Association when he became its president in 1907.

Looking like something out of a fairytale – all turrets, towers and gothic arches – Lowther Castle was once the family home. It was built between 1806 and 1811 by Robert Smirke who went on to design the British Museum. Distinguished visitors to the castle included Kaiser Wilhelm II and the Prince of Wales, later Edward VII, but the building proved too much for the Lowthers and they abandoned it in the 1930s. All that remains today is a shell, but there are ambitious plans to turn the site into a visitor attraction.

Keep to the road for the next 800m, passing St Michael's Church on your left. Soon after drawing level with **Lowther Castle** up to the right, turn left along a

Askham

private, sealed lane with public right of way for pedestrians. When the track splits, bear right, keeping to the high ground above the river.

The surfaced track ends at Buckholme Lodge, but continue in the same direction beyond the gate. You are now on a grassy track with Clifton straight ahead and the North Pennines beyond. Having crossed the field, the track swings right. As it does so, leave it by crossing the stile in the fence, effectively continuing in the same direction. ◄

There are a couple of standing stones a little way up the track to the right, clearly visible from the stile.

The track reaches the side of the **M6** and then swings left to run alongside the motorway for a few hundred metres. Walk under the railway line and then swing right to cross the M6 via Clifton Hall Bridge.

All that remains of **Clifton Hall** is a pele tower, built in the 15th century, which stands alone in the farmyard. It is the sole surviving part of the manor house of

the Wybergh family, and was plundered by Jacobites in 1745 before the Battle of Clifton Moor (see below). It is in the care of English Heritage, and information panels help visitors understand the layout of the buildings to which it was once attached.

Pele towers are unique to the area along the Scottish border. With walls between 3ft and 10ft thick, they were designed to protect families during cross-border raids. The ground floor was used as a storage area, where animals could also be kept, while the first and second floors formed the cooking and living areas.

On the other side of the bridge, turn right through the kissing-gate to walk with a wall on your left. Once over the next stile, turn left to continue alongside the wall. Walk through a fenced area and then swing left. Go through the large gate on the right and head for a gap in the high wall near St Cuthbert's Church on the edge of **Clifton**.

The pele tower at Clifton

Clifton was the site of the last battle on English soil. It took place on 18 December 1745 when about a thousand of Bonnie Prince Charlie's retreating Jacobite rebels clashed with the Duke of Cumberland's forces. Lord George Murray, one of the Jacobite's most competent officers, was leading the group and, by engaging the government troops, acted against Prince Charlie's orders to withdraw and make for Carlisle. The dozen or so Highlanders who were killed are said to be buried under the Rebels' Oak, a large tree behind the George and Dragon pub in the village. There is also a small monument in St Cuthbert's churchyard, to the right of the entrance, to the dragoons who died.

Cross the road and turn left to walk along the pavement. With Penrith and Beacon Hill straight ahead, continue along the **A6** for about 1.5km.

Soon after passing the sign heralding your arrival in **Eamont Bridge**, cross the River Lowther. Turn left immediately after the bridge, along the asphalt driveway of Lowther Holiday Park. You soon pass under the **M6** and then a **railway viaduct**.

After passing – and ignoring – a lane heading uphill to the right, you reach the **caravan park**. Keep to the wide track along the right-hand edge of the site, ignoring any tracks to the left. Eventually, you will come to a gate which provides access to a pretty woodland lane beside the river.

The cute, fluffy-tailed and increasingly rare **red squirrel** can still be found in mixed woodland throughout the Eden catchment area. In most of the rest of England and Wales it has been replaced by its grey cousin, introduced from North America in 1876. Greys breed rapidly, with two litters a year, and eat similar food to reds, so they out-compete the reds; the two species tend not to co-exist. Red squirrels are also more susceptible to certain diseases, particularly the devastating squirrel-pox virus, and find it more difficult to adapt when habitats are destroyed.

St Cuthbert's Church, Clifton

Turn right immediately before the humpback bridge over the **River Lowther**. The path, narrow at first, quickly climbs the steep embankment, providing a good view across to Lowther Castle. After the path becomes more track-like, and just before you draw level with the church on the other side of the river, turn sharp right along a waymarked trail. Once over the ladder stile, turn half-left to walk diagonally across the field. Cross the stile in the corner and turn left along a track.

Having passed **Askham Hall** on your left, you re-emerge in the village opposite the Punchbowl Inn. Turn right along the road and retrace your steps to the car park in **Askham**. ▶

Askham Hall is an Elizabethan mansion built around a 14th-century pele tower. It has been the home of the Lowthers since they abandoned Lowther Castle.

89

WALK 13

Flakebridge Wood and Dufton Ghyll

Distance	8¾ miles (14km)
Total ascent	323m (1060ft)
Start/finish	Car park in Dufton (NY 689 249)
Terrain	Farmland, tracks, quiet roads and woodland paths
Walking time	4¼ hrs
Grade	2
Maps	OS Explorer OL19 or OS Landranger 91
Transport	Dufton is served by buses 625 and 573
Refreshments	The Stag Inn, Dufton

Strolling across farmland, through woods and alongside becks at the base of the Pennines near Dufton makes for a wonderful day out at any time of the year, but this walk is at its very best during the bluebell season. Flakebridge Wood is one of the best places in Cumbria to view these beautiful flowers, forming a carpet of blue as far as the eye can see. Dufton Ghyll, too, is a gorgeous location, full of colour in the spring as winter aconite, wood anemones, bluebells and pignut burst into flower.

Leaving the car park in **Dufton**, turn right along the road and then immediately right again, along a track beside the caravan site. This drops into Dufton Ghyll. As it swings right, turn left along a narrow path and cross the footbridge. Once over the beck, turn left to follow it upstream.

Turn left at the road and then immediately right over a stile. Follow the tiny beck on your right and, just after crossing it, go through a stile to access a track. Head towards the farm at **Greenhow** and go through the gate into the yard. Now swing left along a concrete track, keeping to the left of the farm building. When the track, muddier now, swings right, go through the gate in the wall. Continue in roughly the same direction, through another gate. Walk with the wall on your left, going over

Dufton Ghyll

or through several stiles as you cross a series of fields tucked in at the very base of the Pennines. ▶ When you pass a fingerpost next to the wall, continue towards Flakebridge, with the wall on your left

If you look to your left, you are looking straight up the Pennine escarpment. Over to the right are the Lake District fells.

until it swings left. Now bear right, keeping close to the base of a slope on the right. Once over the Keisley Beck footbridge, cross the stile to your left and then bear right to pick up the line of a wall for a short while. When this wall swings away to the right, continue in the same direction as before to cross a stile in a wall at the top of the field. Keep following the same line in the next field. Beyond the next stile, bear half-left to drop to cross a ladder stile in the field corner.

A narrow path swings right to join a track along which you turn right. At a crossing of ways, go straight over, heading gently uphill through the woods. In spring these woods are full of bluebells. As you approach a fenced compound, turn right, following a narrow, waymarked trail. Bear left at a faint fork.

The UK is now home to several different types of **bluebell**. The ones you see in woods, hedges and other shady places tend to be the familiar native bluebell, known as wild hyacinth in Scotland. The Spanish bluebell was introduced to gardens many years ago and

Bluebells in Flakebridge Wood

is sometimes now also found in the countryside. A hybrid, which is seen as a potential threat to the native plant, is now more common than its Spanish parent.

Turn right when you reach a wide track at **Flakebridge.** At the edge of the woods, turn right again. Walk with a fence on your left for about 800m, abandoning the track when it swings right in a short while. Beyond a stile, continue with the fence on your right.

Go through a gate providing access to a grassy track known as Frith Lane. This goes past the farm at **Esplandhill** to reach a road along which you turn right. In about 50m cross a stile partly hidden by hedges on the left. Follow the line of the fence on your right and then keep to the left of the farm buildings.

Turn right along the next road. Soon after passing the 'Brampton' village sign, go through a gate on the left. The faint path passes to the right of a small stone building. Having crossed a stile over a wall and fence, walk gently uphill with a fence on your left. When this turns sharp left, continue in the same south-westerly direction as before. Aim for a black shed at **Croft Ends** and go through the small gate in front of it. Walk along the track to the left of the farm and then turn left at the road.

Take the next track turning on your right, through **Keld** and over the railway. This track eventually ends at a gate; go through to continue in the same direction. After the next gate, walk with the fence on your left. After the stile, drop to a gate to the left of some sheds to enter the farmyard at **Far Broom**. Pass to the right of a large green tank and then to the left of the farmhouse.

A concrete track takes you all the way to the road, along which you turn right. After 140m go through the stile on your left. Walk with the fence on your left and then, beyond the next gate, bear half-left across the field to reach a stile in a fence. Once over this, head down to the beck and then bear right.

Turn left at the road and then take the first road turning on your right in **Long Marton**. After passing under the railway, and soon after a row of cottages, turn right

Ewes and their lambs seek shade under a tree

through a gate. Beyond the next gate, make for a third gate straight ahead. Now bear slightly right, towards a bend in the beck. Continue in the same direction to a stile. After crossing some damp ground, you reach a second stile, beyond which you turn left.

Go through the gate and turn right along a rough track. Keep straight ahead through several gates. The gates are soon replaced by stiles and, after crossing a stile next to Mill Beck, bear half-left towards a lightly wooded slope. Bearing right again, follow the base of this, keeping almost parallel with the beck over to the right. As the ground to your left becomes less steep, the right-of-way veers more towards the beck. Crossing several stiles along the way and ignoring one bridge, follow the beck upstream for about 1km.

Turn right at the road and then, almost immediately after crossing the beck, go through the gate on your right to enter Dufton Ghyll woods. The path follows Mill Beck downstream for a short while, but then swings left to cross a footbridge.

This **woodland** is classed as semi-natural ancient woodland. Managed by the Woodland Trust, the charity began to replant native species such as oak, rowan and ash in the 1980s. The woods contain several dis-used quarries from which St Bees sandstone was once extracted.

You are now in Dufton Ghyll proper. Keep to the main path, climbing gently. Ignore one path off to the left and then go straight over a shady crossing of paths. Turn left at a junction with a track and head downhill. Follow this track over the beck, round to the left and back to the road in **Dufton**.

WALK 14
Dufton Pike

Distance	4 miles (6.6km)
Total ascent	326m (1070ft)
Start/finish	Car park in Dufton (NY 689 249)
Terrain	Farmland, grassy ridge path and tracks
Walking time	3hrs
Grade	3
Maps	OS Explorer OL19 or OS Landranger 91
Transport	Dufton is served by buses 625 and 573
Refreshments	The Stag Inn, Dufton

Dufton Pike is the conical fell that seems to tower over the East Fellside village of Dufton. But at just 481m (1578ft) its 'towering' nature is an illusion, and its ridges are nowhere near as steep as they appear from the village. A walk along the full length of the pike's mostly grassy spine makes for a lovely and relatively straightforward excursion.

Leaving the car park, turn left and walk along the main road through **Dufton**.

The pretty red sandstone village of **Dufton**, which is built around a long green and an avenue of lime trees,

95

Dufton Pike

has a hall and cottages dating back to the 16th and 17th centuries. During the 18th century the Quaker-owned London Lead Company took control of lead mining in the area and soon began building cottages for its workers and their families in the village. They also provided Dufton with a school, a library and piped water.

Having left the village and passed a turning on the left, the road bends left. Leave it here by turning right, along a wide track towards **Coatsyke Farm**. This is known as Hurning Lane and it soon joins the Pennine Way.

As you go through the farm-yard, keep to the left of the main

96

group of buildings. Continue along the muddy track with the field boundary on your left. You leave the confines of the tree-lined lane when you reach the abandoned farmhouse at Halsteads. The more open track now climbs gently on to Cosca Hill where you get a good view across to Knock Pike.

Continue downhill until you reach a gate in the valley bottom. Do not go through this; instead, continue on the southern side of the stream, along a gently rising track. This hidden valley, home to **Great Rundale Beck**, sees little sun in the winter, but it is a lovely spot in the spring and summer when the leaves and blossom return to its stunted trees, which include hazel and hawthorn.

Go through one gate/stile in a drystone wall followed soon after by another stile in a wall. Straight after this second wall turn sharp right, straight up the fell along a narrow, grassy path. This climbs alongside the wall and then joins a wider track coming in from the left. You quickly reach a high point where you can see across the Eden Valley and to the Lake District beyond. Now turn left to head straight up Dufton Pike's wide, grassy ridge.

Looking into Great Rundale from the top of Dufton Pike

To the south are Wild Boar Fell and the Howgills, and Cross Fell looms to the north.

The route gets a bit steeper as you approach the top, but before you know it, the hard work is over and you are rewarded with the sight of hills in all directions. The Lake District has been visible since joining the ridge. Looking down the line of the Pennine chain, Murton Pike stands out as another conical top sitting at the base of the higher fells. ◄

As you begin descending south-east at first you will see a faint trail along the very highest point of the ridge, but there is a more obvious path slightly to the right of the high ground that follows an easier line. This plummets to a kissing-gate, beyond which you turn right along a clear track. As you reach the edge of **Dufton**, walk straight ahead on the road. It soon swings right and, just after it does so, you will see the car park on the left.

WALK 15

High Cup

Distance	10 miles (15.9km)
Total ascent	674m (2210ft)
Start/finish	Car park in Dufton (NY 689 249)
Terrain	Good tracks and boggy, pathless moorland
Walking time	5½ hrs
Grade	4
Maps	OS Explorer OL19 or OS Landranger 91
Transport	Dufton is served by buses 625 and 573
Refreshments	The Stag Inn, Dufton

High Cup is one of the most famous sights in the North Pennines, a line of exposed dolerite (part of the Great Whin Sill) that forms a spectacular rim around the steep-sided, forbidding valley of High Cup Gill. This route approaches it via the bleak but beautiful moorland to the south-east of Great Rundale Tarn. The paths up here are faint at best, but the tarn's outlet stream acts as a reliable guide for much of the way.

Leaving the car park in **Dufton**, turn right and follow the road as it bends left. When it then bends right, walk up the lane between the sandstone buildings straight ahead. Having ignored the track that bears left around the back of the buildings, stride out down the pleasant lane, soon passing the turning for the Pennine Way on your left. Eventually you leave farmland behind as you reach a pair of gates providing access to more open country at the foot of **Dufton Pike**. Before long, pleasant, rolling landscape formed by the Pennine foothills is replaced by a more rugged aspect as the track heads up into **Great Rundale**, enclosed by steep rock walls and the remains of old mine workings. ▸

Lead was mined in Great Rundale from the 18th century until about 1900 followed by barytes extraction until the mid-1920s. The dumps were also worked for a while in the 1980s.

Despite what it says on some maps, the track continues all the way to the 'shooting box' on the moors proper. This, at 678m (2224ft), is the highest point on the walk. Immediately after the shooting box, turn right along a stream bed to reach **Great Rundale Tarn**. Bearing left at the water's edge, walk around the side of this peaceful, peaty pool until you reach its outlet stream, ignoring a tempting vehicle-wide track heading off to the left.

Great Rundale Tarn

This outlet stream is the key to the next section of the walk, which crosses wild, remote Pennine moorland. You must follow it for the next 2.2km, until you reach Maizebeck Bridge. The best way to begin is to cross the outlet stream at the tarn and follow a narrow, but fairly solid path downstream for a while, but whichever side you choose you end

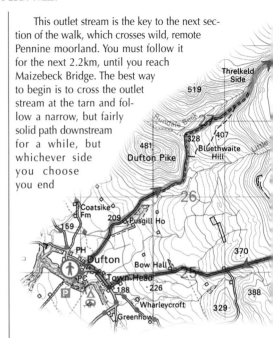

up criss-crossing the main channel for the first 800m or so. There are faint paths on the ground at times, especially where there are grouse butts nearby, but what is a fairly straightforward stroll in a dry summer or hard frost becomes a soggy, peaty mess in wet weather. After the first 800m the best option is to keep to the north-east side of the beck.

Eventually you reach **Maizebeck Bridge**, which crosses the deep dark gorge below. Once over, make for the stone pillar just 10m ahead and then bear left (SSW) along a faint path. Take care here because the path is not always clear. Your bearing becomes more south-westerly as you head across the flat expanse of **High Cup Plain**. You will know when you have arrived at **High Cup** itself: the ground ahead suddenly drops away and you are greeted by a truly breathtaking sight.

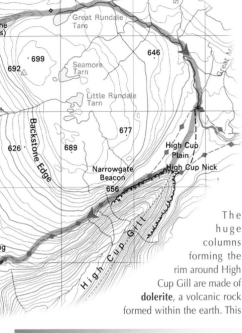

The huge columns forming the rim around High Cup Gill are made of **dolerite**, a volcanic rock formed within the earth. This

High Cup Gill

101

Exposed dolerite columns along the rim of High Cup Gill

igneous rock was squeezed in between two layers of limestone following volcanic eruptions, probably in southern Scotland, many millions of years ago. The columns formed as the dolerite then cooled and shrank.

This layer of dolerite is known as the Great Whin Sill and forms a line through the North Pennines and Northumberland as far as Lindisfarne. Several castles and much of Hadrian's Wall are built on top of the Great Whin Sill, the resulting cliffs forming an extra line of defence against attack.

Turn right along a clear, grassy path a few metres back from the edge of the escarpment. In 450m, just before the main path starts to rise, bear left to follow an interesting path that sticks to a wide, natural ledge with steep drops down to the left. Having carefully forded a shallow but slippery beck, either continue along this ledge path or use the partly constructed path a few metres back from the edge. Before long they join up, and eventually you make your way down through some unusual limestone outcrops and shake-holes to a gate. Once over the stile beside it, stride out along the clear track heading gently downhill with lovely views across to the Lake District.

There is a slight sense of disappointment when the rough track turns to asphalt and you know that your long day on the fells is coming to an end. Turn right at a T-junction and follow the road back into **Dufton**.

WALK 16
Mayburgh Henge and Brougham Castle

Distance	3¾ miles (6.1km)
Total ascent	61m (200ft)
Start/finish	Parking area for Eden Millennium Monument just to the west of Eamont Bridge (NY 520 282). If coming from the A66, drive through Eamont Bridge, turn right at the small roundabout near The Crown pub and then take the second lane on the right. The parking area is on the left as the lane bends to the right.
Terrain	Field and riverside paths, some road walking
Walking time	1¾ hrs
Grade	1
Maps	OS Explorer OL5 or OS Landranger 90
Transport	Eamont Bridge is served by buses 108 and 106
Refreshments	Fusion Café, Brougham Hall; Beehive Inn and The Crown at Eamont Bridge

The area around Eamont Bridge is littered with historical sites, and this short walk visits no fewer than five of them, spanning thousands of years of human occupation: two prehistoric henges, a Roman fort, a 13th-century castle and an old fortified hall. The going underfoot is generally easy as you follow well-waymarked paths, a pretty riverside trail and quiet country lanes.

From the parking area just outside **Eamont Bridge**, walk north-west along the lane. To visit **Mayburgh Henge**, go through the kissing-gate on the right.

The solitary stone in the centre of Mayburgh Henge

Mayburgh Henge is a large and impressive Neolithic circular bank built of stones taken from the river, which is up to 6.4m high in places. Once you've climbed the embankment you will see a single standing stone, close to its centre. Sketches from the 18th century suggest the stone was one of a group of four. Other records suggest there may even have been two stone circles within the enclosure.

Continuing the walk, go back through the kissing-gate and turn right along the lane. Just after passing Southwaite Green Cottages, climb the stone stile on the right. The path is fenced on both sides at first. When you reach a gap on your right, make sure you keep to the left of the fence. Go through the kissing-gate near Bleach Mill and bear right along the asphalt track beside the **River Eamont**.

Cross straight over the road and go through the small gate opposite. Turn left to cross the footbridge over the river and then turn right along a clear riverside track. When you reach the gates of the private residence at Low Mill, cross the wooden stile on your left and then a second stile a few metres beyond.

The clear, waymarked trail swings right, through a narrow band of trees, and then crosses another stile to regain the river bank, where you have a good chance of seeing herons.

▶ Having crossed one gated bridge and some stiles along the way, keep to the riverside path until you reach a fence near a small cottage. Follow the fence round to the left and then strike off across the field to a stile in the fence on the other side. Once over this, turn right along the surfaced lane and then right again at the T-junction. You soon recross the **River Eamont** and pass the entrance to **Brougham Castle**, which you will have been able to see across the river.

The building on the other side of the field here is Carleton Hall, Cumbria Police headquarters.

Brougham Castle

BROUGHAM CASTLE

The ruins of medieval Brougham (pronounced 'Broom') Castle are located on the banks of the River Eamont, near the site of a Roman fort. The 13th-century keep, built by Robert de Vieuxpont, survives, as do many of the buildings added by the powerful Clifford family in the 14th century.

The Cliffords played host to both James I and Charles I here, but the castle was in a poor condition by the time of the Civil War. Then Lady Anne Clifford came along (see Walk 4), and it became one of the many castles and churches that she restored. It also eventually became her main residence and she died here in 1676.

The castle is in the care of English Heritage today, but is closed from October until the end of March. There is an admission fee.

At the next crossroads, turn right.

Looking to your right, you will see the earthwork remains of a **Roman fort** that guarded the ford. Known in Roman times as Brocavum, it was built in AD76 and would have been manned by about a thousand soldiers. This would also have been the northern terminus of High Street, the high-level Roman road that once linked this fort with one near Ambleside, at the northern end of Windermere. An exhibition at the nearby castle includes stones from the fort.

When the road forks, bear right towards Pooley Bridge and Ullswater, and you soon start climbing gently towards **Brougham Hall**. As you approach the old hall, follow the road round to the right. Drop down between high walls and under a bridge linking the hall with a small church.

Brougham Hall is thought to occupy the site of a fortified house dating from the 14th century. The hall became famous in Victorian times when it was home to the Lord Chancellor and was known as the 'Windsor of the north'. Situated almost exactly half-way between Windsor and Balmoral, it played host to royalty. Today

This door knocker at Brougham Hall is a 20th-century replica of the 12th-century original

it is home to craft workshops, a café and several other small businesses.

Turn right at the main road and then left at the mini-roundabout on the edge of **Eamont Bridge**. To visit King Arthur's Round Table go through the kissing-gate in the wall on the left. Otherwise, continue along the road and take the second turning on the right, towards Southwaite Green. The parking area is just a few metres ahead.

King Arthur's Round Table is a circular enclosure with a surrounding ditch and causeways. Like Mayburgh, it dates from prehistoric times, but sadly this henge has been badly damaged by road-building. Legend has it that this was King Arthur's jousting arena.

WALK 17

Culgaith and Acorn Bank

Distance	6¾ miles (11km)
Total ascent	192m (630ft)
Start/finish	Black Swan Inn, Culgaith (NY 607 296). Please park considerately nearby in the village
Terrain	Riverside paths, farmland and country roads
Walking time	3¼ hrs
Grade	1–2
Maps	OS Explorer OL19 and OL5 or OS Landranger 91
Transport	Culgaith is served by buses 130, 135, 138, 140 and 562
Refreshments	Black Swan Inn, Culgaith; teashop at Acorn Bank (open Wednesday to Sunday, April to end of October)

A chance to visit two lovely Eden Valley villages, Culgaith and Temple Sowerby, as well as the National Trust's Acorn Bank. Here you can wander through delightful woods that are home to red squirrels and visit the restored mill buildings. The gardens are also open to the public, but there is an entrance fee for non-members.

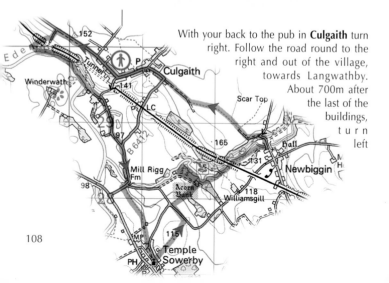

With your back to the pub in **Culgaith** turn right. Follow the road round to the right and out of the village, towards Langwathby. About 700m after the last of the buildings, turn left

along a farm track, signposted Pea Foot, which provides good views towards the Lake District fells, including Blencathra and the Helvellyn range. After going through a gate just above the **River Eden**, turn left alongside the fence. Go through the kissing-gate to access a lovely riverside path through Hag Wood. This gradually becomes more track-like as it makes its way upstream.

Looking across to the Lake District fells

The track eventually goes through a solid wooden gate to the right of a water treatment works. Turn right along the road on the edge of **Culgaith** and then, after 600m, right again at a T-junction, towards Penrith and Appleby.

About 500m along this road, having crossed **Crowdundle Beck**, you will see a turning on the left to Newbiggin, Milburn and Acorn Bank. Cross the stile at this junction and then walk beside a tiny beck on your left. The path comes away from the beck slightly after the next stile, but continue walking parallel with the line of trees/fence. After a few more stiles you pass to the right of another water treatment works and go through

The North Pennines from near Culgaith

a kissing-gate. Cross straight over this field, towards the buildings on the edge of **Temple Sowerby**.

The Knights Templar were early owners of the manor of Sowerby. After they were disbanded by the Pope in the early 14th century, the manor passed into the hands of the Knight Hospitallers

◀ Go through the metal gate in the wall and turn right along the road through the village. Turn left along a residential road opposite the village green and then left again on a track between the houses. (Don't be tempted by the first grassy gap on your left; the track you want has a fingerpost indicating it is a right-of-way to Newbiggin Road.)

Go through a small gate and enter a field. Make your way over to the hedgerow on the left and follow this to the minor road. Turn left and then, as you draw level with a road turning on your left, go through the gate on the right. The path heads to the left of the big red sandstone house at Acorn Bank. Cross the access road in front of the house and go through the small gate opposite. Walk parallel with the fence on the left, through an area of picnic benches.

The handsome house at **Acorn Bank** is not open to the public, but the gardens, contained within 17th-century

The gardens at Acorn Bank are well worth a visit

walls, are. These are home to a massive collection of medicinal and culinary herbs. The orchards are well known for their traditional varieties and there is an 'apple day' every October to celebrate this. The day includes apple bobbing, storytelling, cookery demonstrations, children's music, craft workshops, a treasure hunt, Punch and Judy and Morris dancers.

Turn left along a constructed path through the oak woods. This leads to the restored mill buildings, which are open to the public; there are interpretation panels to explain how the machinery worked. ▶

The path swings round to the right here, alongside the mill race at first. Having crossed a wooden footbridge, bear right at a fork in the path. After the next bridge, the path climbs the embankment to reach a T-junction. Turn left and you soon reach the edge of the National Trust woodland. Cross the wooden stile and continue alongside **Crowdundle Beck**. Occasionally you will pick up faint signs of the path on the muddy ground, but the beck acts as your most dependable

There has been a mill at Acorn Bank, powered by water from nearby Crowdundle Beck, for several centuries, although the current buildings are only 150 years old.

guide. On reaching the next fence, the stile is hidden by a bush right next to the water's edge. Continuing upstream and passing beneath a viaduct, you can see Great Dun Fell straight ahead.

Turn left when you reach the road near **Newbiggin**. When it bends sharp right, turn left. This wide track swings right and then reaches a pair of gates. Cross the stile to the right of the gate straight ahead and follow the track right and then left, around the edge of the field. At the next set of gates, as the track fades away, keep straight ahead with the hedge on your right.

Approaching the far end of this field, swing away from the hedge slightly to pass through a stile in the wall about 30m to the left of a gate. Cut diagonally across this field (WNW) and then continue in the same direction once over the next stile. Cross yet another stile beside the gate in the field corner to access a track between two fences.

River Eden near Culgaith

Keep straight ahead at the road and then follow it round to the left to return to the Black Swan in **Culgaith**.

112

WALK 18
Cross Fell

Distance	10¼ miles (16.6km)
Total ascent	762m (2500ft)
Start/finish	Village hall in Blencarn (NY 638 312). Please park considerately nearby in the village
Terrain	Good paths and tracks on open moorland, wet in places
Walking time	5¾ hrs
Grade	4
Maps	OS Explorer OL31 or OS Landranger 91
Transport	Blencarn is served by buses 130, 135, 138 and 140
Refreshments	Nearest pubs and cafés are in Langwathby, Kirkby Thore, Temple Sowerby and Culgaith

No guide to the Eden Valley would be complete without an ascent of the fell that seems to loom over much of this area. At 893m (2929ft), Cross Fell is the highest point along the entire Pennine chain, and it dominates the view on many of the walks in this book. There are several ways to reach this wild, windswept top, and none of them is short; this route from Blencarn is probably the shortest and most straightforward of them all. It ascends a mostly clear, grassy bridleway that gradually climbs all the way to the source of the River Tees. From here, it joins the Pennine Way to cross the large flat summit with its expansive views. The descent is via another mostly clear track.

With your back to **Blencarn** village hall turn left, and when the road bends right keep straight ahead towards a gate beyond the last of the houses. Go through this and swing left along the rough track. Ignoring another track off to the right early on, this strip of access land, contained within two drystone walls, soon begins to narrow. The path mostly keeps close to the wall on the right after passing close by a small farm shed, but patches of gorse force it to deviate from this line from time to time.

About 500m after passing the public byway off to the left near the house at **Wythwaite**, go through two gates in quick succession to access open land at the base of the

113

Ponies grazing near Blencarn

fells. Using a wide, grassy path through the bracken, keep close to Littledale Beck on your right. Ford the beck and then continue upstream towards the **Grumply Hill**.

At the base of the hill, ignore the path going steeply uphill to the right; simply keep following the clear, grassy bridleway as it heads further up into the valley.

The ascent is reasonably steady at first, but then becomes steeper as the bridleway suddenly does a left turn to climb across the front of **Wildboar Scar**. Keep to the clearest path as you wind your way up through an area littered with piles of boulders. The gradient then eases considerably and you get a good view of Little Dun and Great Dun fells to the east. ◀

The golfball-like contraption on Great Dun Fell is part of the Civil Aviation Authority's air traffic control radar.

The ground can be soggy in places as you approach Tees Head and it is easy to lose the path temporarily in the quagmire. There are, however, cairns to guide you as you head north-east. When you reach the paved ridge path, which is the route of the Pennine Way, turn left. ▶

This is the **English watershed**; all becks flowing west of this ridge end up in the Irish Sea and everything to the east goes to the North Sea. One of the great rivers of the North, the Tees, has its source here. It plummets down through the Pennines via the waterfalls at Cauldron Snout and High Force, meanders its way through County Durham and reaches the sea just beyond Stockton and Middlesbrough, about 85 miles from where it started.

As the flagstones run out keep heading straight up the slope, and eventually you will reach the first in a line of tall cairns that guide you across the

This area of the Pennines is known for its Arctic/Alpine plants, such as the spring gentian. They colonised the area after the last Ice Age and have survived ever since.

One of the cairns marking the route on Cross Fell

As befits the highest point along 'England's backbone', the view is magnificent: a long line of Lake District fells, the Cheviots and, on a clear day, the Dumfries and Galloway hills.

substantial summit plateau (WNW). The top of **Cross Fell** is marked by a trig pillar and a large shelter. ◀

From the shelter follow the cairned path, first north and then veering slightly left. As you drop down the northern side of the fell, pass to the right of **Crossfell Well**, beyond which the going gets decidedly soggy. It is hard to make out the path here, but as long as you head roughly NNW you will eventually return to dry land as you reach a wide, clear track.

This track was once a '**corpse road**'. Before the churchyard in Garrigill was consecrated, villagers used to have to carry their dead over the Pennines to Kirkland for burial at St Lawrence's Church. Corpse roads used to be a common occurrence in Cumbria, and there are famous examples between Wasdale and Eskdale, near Grasmere, and at Loweswater. They frequently crossed bleak and lonely fells and, inevitably, are often associated with ghost stories.

Turn left and the long descent to Kirkland soon begins with some great views across the patchwork of fields that make up the Eden Valley to the Lake District beyond. The track can best be described as intermittent in its early stages. Its general direction is WSW until it reaches some disused **mine workings**. Then it becomes a lot clearer as it begins to wind its way downhill.

Having gone through several gates and passed **Kirkland Hall**, the track becomes a surfaced lane. At the junction close to the church in Kirkland, keep straight ahead towards Blencarn. About 500m beyond the junction go through a signposted gate on your left. The right-of-way cuts south diagonally across this field. As you approach an area of trees, keep to the top of a small ridge of land with the fence on your left. Cross a stile and follow the narrow trail through a small area of woodland and over another stile. Walk with the fence on your left and then, immediately after a footbridge, cross the stile on your left. Continue in the same direction as before, but this time with the fence on your right.

Descending the old 'corpse road' to Kirkland

On approaching the edge of the fishing pond, follow the fence round to the left and then, when you reach a wall, go through the gate on the right. When the fence over to your right kinks right, make your way over to it and follow it until you reach a gate. Now turn sharp left and walk uphill to a gate in a fence. Once through this, walk with the fence on your right and then go through the gate in the field corner on the edge of **Blencarn**. Follow the gravel track to the road and turn left to return to the village hall.

WALK 19

Long Meg and Lacy's Caves

Distance	5½ miles (8.7km)
Total ascent	223m (730ft)
Start/finish	Little Salkeld Watermill (NY 566 360). Please park considerately nearby in the village
Terrain	Riverside path, tracks and quiet lanes
Walking time	2½ hrs
Grade	1–2
Maps	OS Explorer OL5 or OS Landranger 90 and 91
Transport	Little Salkeld is served by buses 131, 135, 137 and 139
Refreshments	Little Salkeld Watermill's tearoom, open daily 10.30am–5pm except Christmas and New Year

You should allow plenty of time for sightseeing and general dawdling on this sublime walk through some of the Eden Valley's prettiest countryside. The route visits a water-powered corn mill, a lonely church that has lost its village, fascinating caves carved into sandstone cliffs and, probably the highlight of the excursion, one of the most impressive and mysterious stone circles in the whole of Britain. And as if all that wasn't enough, there is a lovely riverside path and the chance of seeing red squirrels – all for relatively little effort.

With your back to the watermill in **Little Salkeld**, turn right along the road and then follow it round to the right, towards Glassonby and Gamblesby. Having climbed gently, turn left on to a rough track and then follow it round to the right. Just before you reach **Long Meg and Her Daughters** a sign on the right, indicating a bridleway to Glassonby, points to a field corner with three gates in it. This is your onward route after the obligatory exploration of the stone circle.

LONG MEG AND HER DAUGHTERS

This is probably one of the most enigmatic sites in the whole of Cumbria. This huge stone circle, which has a road running through it, consists of 59 stones, although originally there were about 70. The largest stone is Long Meg herself, a 12ft-tall standing stone that bears faint traces of mysterious cup and ring markings as well as concentric circles, which are thought to be 4500 years old. Constructed of red sandstone quarried from the banks of the River Eden, she is positioned just outside the circle. Seen from the centre of the circle, she is aligned with the midwinter sunset.

Needless to say, there are a lot of spooky local legends associated with this atmospheric site. The stones are said to be the petrified remains of a coven of witches who were turned to stone by Scottish wizard Michael Scot for profanities on the Sabbath. The site is supposedly endowed with ▶

magic, so that it is impossible to count the same number of stones twice. If you do manage to do so, then the magic is broken (or, alternatively, you are cursed by bad luck).

A prophecy also states that if Long Meg were ever to be shattered, she would run with blood. It is said that when local squire Colonel Lacy attempted to destroy the stones in the 18th century, a terrifying storm broke out and the labourers fled in fear of Black Magic, and refused to return.

Having explored the site, take the Glassonby bridleway. Go through the small wooden gate with a yellow waymarker on it to walk with the fence and hedgerow on your immediate right. On the other side of the field, choose the right-hand of the two metal gates and then go straight through the small wooden gate on the other side of the track.

Walking with field boundaries on your left, pass through a series of gates until you reach a rough farm track. Once through the metal gate on the other side, make for the small gate in the church wall opposite.

St Michael and All Angels, Addingham, was built on its present site in the 13th century. The original church and village were washed away when the River Eden changed course in the 12th century. A Norse hogsback tombstone, two pieces of a cross shaft and some early coffin lids are kept in the church porch. They were retrieved from the site of the original church during a drought in 1913. A 10th-century wheel-headed Anglian cross in the churchyard is also thought to have come from the earlier church.

St Michael and All Angels, Addingham

Leave the churchyard via the heavy metal gates on the other side of the building, and turn left down a rough track. This ends at a junction of paths where you turn right. Eventually, the delightful grassy lane narrows to become a footpath passing to the right of a metal gate.

Drop down to the road just to the right of the path-end and turn left. On reaching Daleraven Bridge, which crosses a tributary of the River Eden, turn left along a footpath, quickly climbing an embankment to cross a stile in a fence. Bearing half-right, you are soon brought to a sudden halt as you find yourself standing on the edge of a steep precipice looking down on the serene **River Eden**.

What follows now as you bear left is a peaceful riverside stroll, sometimes across grassy meadows, sometimes through pretty woodland where you have a good chance of spotting red squirrels. After walking 1.2km from Daleraven Bridge, you reach an area of sandstone cliffs. Immediately after the path drops down a flight of steps, you can take a detour by turning right along a narrow path that goes through a cleft in the rocks. This brings you to **Lacy's Caves**, but be careful here because some of the caves open out on to precipitous drops. ▶

This is not a place for dogs or unsupervised children.

121

Lacy's Caves

The same **Colonel Lacy** who attempted to destroy Long Meg and Her Daughters was responsible for these impressive caverns, hollowed out of the red sandstone embankments of the river. He created the five chambers in an attempt to impress his guests, and supposedly even employed a man to live there and pretend to be a hermit.

Continuing along the main riverside path, you soon pass the remains of the gypsum mine.

Gypsum mining started here in 1870, first from the surface and later moving underground, for use in the production of plaster. In the 1920s, following a brief period of closure, the mine was used to supply anhydrite to fertiliser manufacturers. The mining of gypsum and anhydrite is now confined to the Kirkby Thore area of the Eden Valley.

After passing in front of an electricity sub-station, turn right along a concrete track and right again soon afterwards, following signs for Little Salkeld. The track

The restored watermill in Little Salkeld

123

ends at a T-junction, where you turn left. Turn right at the main road junction to return to the watermill in **Little Salkeld**.

> This working **corn mill** still uses water power and traditional techniques to produce a range of stone-ground organic flours. Originally built in 1745, it started life as a modest affair but then prospered when the Carlisle–Settle railway line was built.
>
> The gorgeous buildings were lovingly restored by Ana and Nick Jones in 1975. They and their enthusiastic team run guided tours of the site, and the full range of flours is on sale next door in the delightful café. Visitors are advised to phone in advance (Tel. 01768 881523) because guided tours may not be available if the mill is busy. Self-guided tours are also possible.

WALK 20

Melmerby Fell

Distance	8¾ miles (14.2km)
Total ascent	616m (2020ft)
Start/finish	Melmerby village (NY 615 373)
Terrain	Tracks and open pathless moorland, wet in places
Walking time	5hrs
Grade	4
Maps	OS Explorer OL31 or OS Landranger 91
Transport	Melmerby is served by buses 130, 139, 140 and 888
Refreshments	The Village Bakery and the Shepherd's Inn, Melmerby

This route sets off from the lovely red sandstone village of Melmerby to climb its eponymous fell via quiet lanes and a lovely grassy track. You will hardly see a soul as you wander the wide open spaces above the Eden Valley; apart from the sheep, the only company you are likely to have are the curlews, the skylarks and the occasional golden plover. And if you enjoyed your time on the tops, just wait for the descent! A beautiful green lane winds its way down through a series of fine knobbly hills with views across to the distant Lake District.

From the centre of **Melmerby** and with the Shepherd's Inn

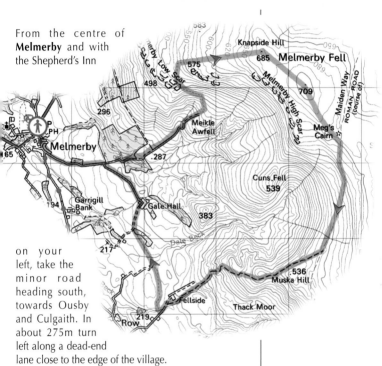

on your left, take the minor road heading south, towards Ousby and Culgaith. In about 275m turn left along a dead-end lane close to the edge of the village.

Having climbed for about 800m, the lane swings right. Leave it here by keeping straight ahead on a rough track between two drystone walls. The track winds its way through woodland and then emerges to a wonderful view of the steep western edge of the Pennine escarpment.

Eventually go through a gate and then climb to the final wall before reaching the open fell. The track soon makes a wide swing to the left and recrosses the wall higher up the fell. The track then bears right again near

125

Pockets of snow linger on Melmerby Fell

Gate Castle, which makes up part of **Melmerby Low Scar**. After this, keep right at any forks in the track.

Go through a gate in the wall and head eastwards towards the prominent cairn straight ahead; then continue east towards the cairn on the skyline marking the top of **Knapside Hill**. The terrain now consists of a combination of grassy tufts, moss and dank green pools. You also pass several shake holes as you make your way to the summit. ◄

From the top, you get your first view to the east, across the wide, largely uninhabited expanse of the North Pennines.

Head south-east along a faint path towards the next cairn on top of Dun Edge which, at 709m (2326ft), is the highest point on **Melmerby Fell**. Swing slightly south along the high ground, and when you reach a wall corner continue in the same direction, keeping the wall on your right. Go through the next gate in the wall to pick up a faint grassy track.

This track marks the route of the **Maiden Way**, one of the highest Roman roads in the country. As well as being used to gain access to the lead mines of Alston Moor, this road from Bewcastle to Kirkby Thore also cut through the Briganteum region. The Brigantes were a

On the Maiden Way

powerful native people who lived in this area and the Romans are thought to have used the road to exert control over them.

The track heads southwards at first, but eventually swings south-west as it gently descends. ▶ There is a cairn to guide you just after the first gate. About 225m beyond the second gate, just after a wall corner, bear right at a fork. Before long this track swings right, so that you walk with a fence on your right.

For the next 2km or so, you follow what has to be one of the loveliest green lanes in the whole of the Pennines. The view of the secluded valley of Ousbydale down to your right and of steep-sided Cuns Fell is replaced, as you pass through Windy Gap, by far-ranging views to the south. ▶

Soon after passing an intricate set of sheepfolds, the track swings right and you lose the wall on your right for a short while. At the lane-end, go through the gate on your left to join a rough track. This quickly swings right, alongside a wall, and drops into a valley containing Spoutgill Sike. Pass close to the buildings at **Fellside** and,

The track is not always obvious on the ground and several boggy patches add to the difficulties.

All the while, the Lake District fells hold the promise of more rugged walking in the distance.

Looking across Ousbydale to Cuns Fell

after the last of several gates, walk along the stream bed to reach a farm lane.

Go through a gate diagonally opposite to the left. Follow the tiny beck and then, once through the next gate, head uphill with a line of small, knarled trees on the right. Go through the stile on your left at the top and follow the track downhill for a few metres. When the track swings left at the end of the wall, turn right to walk with a fence on your right. Cross the next stile and then continue in roughly the same direction with the fence on your left.

Go through a gate and, just to the right of a pond, take the right-hand of the two gates. Walk with the fence/ wall on your left. Beyond the next stile, head slightly left to cross a bridge. Having climbed the slope, keep the fence on your left. Cross a stile beside a gate and head straight across the next field towards the corner of the woods. Once over the stile, walk up the rough track to join a wider lane coming in from the left. Follow this into the farmyard at **Gale Hall** and then left between the buildings. This track, which you should soon recognise from earlier in the walk, leads back to **Melmerby**.

WALK 21

Raven Beck and Kirkoswald

Distance	10 miles (16.1km)
Total ascent	439m (1440ft)
Start/finish	Methodist Church, Renwick (NY 596 435)
Terrain	Farmland, beckside path and quiet country roads
Walking time	5hrs
Grade	2
Maps	OS Explorer OL5 and OL31 or OS Landranger 86 and 91
Transport	Renwick is served by buses 131, 133, 134 and 137
Refreshments	Fetherston Arms and Crown Inn, both in Kirkoswald

This fairly long but straightforward walk starts from Renwick at the foot of the Pennines and makes its way almost all the way to the banks of the River Eden. It crosses rolling farmland and uses quiet country lanes with great views of the surrounding hills before paying a visit to the attractive red sandstone village of Kirkoswald. Here walkers can drop in on one of the village's two pubs before the delightful walk back along Raven Beck.

Starting from the Methodist Church in **Renwick**, cross the road and go up the lane opposite, towards Outhwaite. When this swings right, leave it by keeping straight ahead on a rough track. After about 300m turn right and cross a stile in a wall. After crossing the ladder stile straight ahead, bear half-right to head towards a wall corner, and then walk with the fence on your left. Continue in the same direction after a stile, but almost immediately after the next one, go through the gap in the wall on the left. Walking through the trees now, continue with the boundary wall/fence on your right.

After leaving the woods, ignore a small gate on your right, but then cross the stile beside the next gate. Follow the rough track down towards the farm buildings at **Outhwaite** and then turn left along the lane.

The walk starts on farmland at the base of the Pennines

Go through a gate beside a large barn with red doors and then swing right, through another gate and down a rough lane. Keep to the track as it swings right and you will soon see Raven Beck for the first time.

Turn left when you reach the road and then right immediately after the bridge, towards Gamblesby and Melmerby. About 400m beyond the bridge go through a gate on the right. Keep close to the field boundary on the right until you reach the buildings at **Huddlesceugh Hall**. Now go through the gate to the right of a huge gate in a sandstone wall. Keep close to the buildings on your left and then continue with a wall on your left.

As the wall becomes a fence, cross a stile and then continue with the wall on your left and over another stile. Walk straight over the next field to go through a gate with a yellow waymarker and then bear half-right towards a fingerpost just visible on the other

130

side of the wall straight ahead. Cross the awkward stile here and then turn left along the quiet lane.

Go straight over at the crossroads, towards Glassonby and Little Salkeld. Having passed an alpaca farm on **Viol Moor** along the way, take the next road turning on your right. Walk along this lane for 1.3km and then turn right along a surfaced track towards **Old Parks**.

Bear left after entering the farmyard and then leave it through the left-hand of the two gates straight ahead. As you go through a second gate, you will see a bird-bath on a small hillock to your left.

The bird-bath is a memorial to the **Rev George Bramwell Evens**, a Minister of the Methodist Church better known as 'Romany of the BBC'. He presented *Out with Romany* on BBC Radio's *Children's Hour* in the 1930s and 1940s,

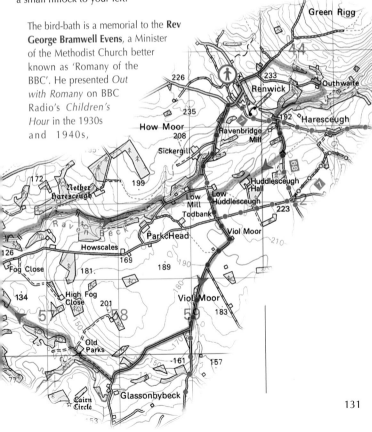

131

and is generally regarded as Britain's first natural history broadcaster. He spent a lot of time at Old Parks Farm watching and studying the wildlife, and his ashes were scattered here after he died in 1943.

An information panel was unveiled by Terry Waite in 2001; however, foot and mouth restrictions prevented it from being moved to its present site next to the path until the following year.

As the track swings left, keep following the fence on your right. Go through a gate and then continue with the fenced area of woodland on your left. After a while a waymarker post will direct you away from the trees and towards a gate to the right of another patch of woodland. Once over the stile beside this gate, cross a second stile to enter the trees. Never stray too far from the fence on your right and eventually cross yet another stile. Walk with the fence on your left and cross the stile next to the gate.

Make your way over to the small fenced hillock straight ahead. Walk with the fence on your left until it kinks sharp left. Continue in the same direction, walking parallel with a fence about 40m to the right. Go through a gate to the right of a pond and, after passing the pond, go through a second gate on to a track between two fences. After a third gate bear left to walk with a fence on your left. You can now see the remains of **Kirkoswald Castle**. Follow the fence round to the right and then cross a stile to access a grassy track.

Turn left along the road and then right at the T-junction. The main route goes right again at the next junction in **Kirkoswald**; however, a short detour to the left will take you to the interesting parish church.

After crossing the bridge over **Raven Beck** in Kirkoswald, turn right along Ravenghyll. ◄ As you reach the top of the lane continue on a path beside the beck. After a couple of gates make sure you keep right at a fork in the path to continue through a lovely area of woodland beside the beck.

You can hear Raven Beck down to the right.

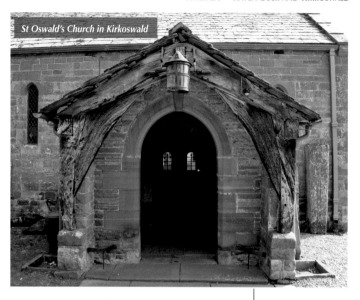
St Oswald's Church in Kirkoswald

KIRKOSWALD

Once a thriving market town, Kirkoswald gets its name from the church of St Oswald. Oswald was the King of Northumbria who travelled around the north of England with St Aidan in the seventh century, trying to convert the inhabitants to Christianity. Local legend has it that St Aidan saw people worshipping at a well here and decided to build a Christian church on top of it. The early church would have been a wooden one, but the current structure dates from 1897. The well is under the nave, but there is access to it on the external west wall, where a metal cup sits attached to a chain. The churchyard also contains some interesting Saxon grave covers.

An unusual feature of St Oswald's is its bell tower, which is actually perched on top of a hill about 140m from the church itself.

Opposite the entrance to the church is the College, a beautiful house originally built as a pele tower in 1450. It was converted into a college for priests by Thomas de Dacre in the 1520s, but was closed in the 1540s following the Dissolution of the Monasteries. It then became the home of the Fetherstonhaugh family, who had previously lived at the castle.

After leaving the trees continue upstream, crossing three fields. As you approach the end of the third one, cross a small bridge on your right followed by a stile. The path is indistinct now, but you should head north-east, away from the water for a short while. As you reach a waymarker at a fork in the path, bear right to reach a kissing-gate. Beyond this you are back on a beckside path through the woods. Ignore the bridge in a short while, keeping the beck on your right as you head upstream.

About 300m after leaving the woods via a stile, finally cross the beck via a wooden footbridge with high railings. Go up the embankment and then turn left along the lane. Having ignored two footpaths on the left, go through a stile in the wall just after a group of cottages at **Low Mill** down to your left. Head north-east diagonally across this field and then cross a wooden stile next to the beck to give access to a permissive path through some saplings.

Turn left at the road and then right at the T-junction, towards Renwick. Follow the road round to the left to return to the Methodist Church in **Renwick**.

Beside Raven Beck

134

WALK 22
Armathwaite and Coombs Wood

Distance	3½ miles (5.8km)
Total ascent	186m (610ft)
Start/finish	Duke's Head Hotel, Armathwaite (NY 505 460)
Terrain	Good tracks and quiet country roads
Walking time	1½ hrs
Grade	1–2
Maps	OS Explorer OL5 or OS Landranger 86
Transport	Armathwaite is on the Settle–Carlisle railway and is served by the 133 and 134 buses
Refreshments	Duke's Head Hotel and Fox and Pheasant Inn, Armathwaite

This makes for a perfect Sunday morning stroll. It starts from one of the loveliest of the Eden Valley's villages and then enters pretty woodland beside the river. Having visited one of Cumbria's more off-the-beaten-track hamlets, Longdales, the route heads along a seemingly forgotten track between hedgerows that are a riot of colour in the early autumn. If you time things carefully, you should arrive back in Armathwaite just in time for pub opening.

Starting with your back to the Duke's Head Hotel in **Armathwaite**, turn right along the road. Immediately after the road bridge over the **River Eden**, cross the stile on the left and follow the path round to the left and under the bridge so that you are heading upstream with the river on your right along a clear, tree-lined path. ▶

Ignoring a couple of narrow trails down to the right, keep to the main path until you draw level with Mill Farm on the other side of some rapids. There is a clear fork here, but, instead of taking either of the two options straight ahead, turn sharp left, almost back on yourself. It is very unclear on the ground, but there is a faint path climbing north-east towards a waymarker post just visible

Look for Armathwaite Castle on the opposite bank. This pele tower was converted into a country house in 1752 by William Sanderson.

The tree-lined path beside the River Eden on the edge of Armathwaite

among the trees. The post marks a junction with a clear path, along which you turn right. Climb easily to a stile in a fence and continue along a wide track through the forest. (You soon pass one of the Eden Benchmark sculptures, 'Vista' by Graeme Mitcheson, carved from St Bees sandstone.)

Another track comes up from the right as you swing left to head deeper into **Coombs Wood**, surrounded by tall, slender conifers. As you approach the end of the forest track, the trees on your right disappear and the wonderful views that you have been snatching tiny glimpses of up until now are suddenly and dramatically revealed. Far below, the River Eden has carved a beautiful valley, the graceful curvy sides of which are covered in woodland and rolling farmland.

Beyond the metal gate, turn left along the road and then take the next road on your right. Immediately after passing the cottages in **Longdales**, turn left along a track. This climbs to a high point of about 170m, from where you get a superb view of the rolling farmland to the north and the Pennines to the east. Those views stay with you as you continue straight ahead between hedgerows.

Turn left along the road. Follow it back across the River Eden and then retrace your steps into **Armathwaite**.

The track heading north from Longdales

Rolling farmland at the foot of the Pennines

WALK 23
Croglin and Newbiggin

Distance	5 miles (8.2km)
Total ascent	220m (720ft)
Start/finish	Croglin (NY 573 471)
Terrain	Tracks, farm paths and quiet country roads
Walking time	2¾ hrs
Grade	2
Maps	OS Explorer OL5 or OS Landranger 86
Transport	Croglin is served by buses 131, 133 and 134
Refreshments	Blue Bell Inn, Newbiggin

In Cumbria the words 'Croglin' and 'vampire' go together like 'Bram' and 'Stoker'. And wandering the tracks and paths linking this tiny fellside settlement with nearby Newbiggin in the depths of winter, it is not hard to see how the story of the Croglin vampire has lingered so long in this bleak but somehow beautiful area tucked in at the very foot of the Pennine escarpment. However, come the spring, the undead couldn't be further from your thoughts as you wander the high track between the two hamlets, listening to the skylarks celebrating the change of season and the ewes calling to their lambs.

Head south-west along the sign-posted track that starts at the former Robin Hood pub in **Croglin**. The track ends at a metal gate to the right of a pond. Go through and head in roughly the same direction, towards a stile in the fence opposite. A faint path then continues through the grass, soon crossing a small beck and climbing to a wall. Walk with the wall on your left until you reach a gate providing access to a quiet road.

Turn right and walk along the asphalt for about nearly 2km, passing a turning on the right for Croglin at **Hazelgill**, and then a turning on theleft. Soon after the latter you will see **Cairnhead Farm** on your right. About 140m beyond these buildings, go through a waymarked gap in the wall up to your right.

Walk with the wall on your left; at the top of the field go through the wooden gate straight ahead and continue with the wall on your left. Cross two stiles followed by a

Looking towards Newbiggin and Cumrew Fells

small beck, beyond which continue with a tumbledown wall on your right. Turn left at the road. Just after passing the pub, turn right to head into **Newbiggin**. Follow this lane almost to its end.

> There are dozens of places called **Newbiggin** all over the north of England, including at least five in the area covered by this guidebook. It simply means 'new building' and originates from Old Norse.

As you approach **Townhead** you will see a track heading up to the left on to access land. Ignore this; continue for just a few more metres to pick up a signposted bridleway that starts just to the left of a house called Brookside.

The views become more and more interesting as you gradually gain height.

The clear wide track climbs at a moderate angle through the wooded ravine. As it emerges from the trees follow it round to the right, ignoring the footpath that goes through the gate straight ahead. ◄ The Northern Fells can be clearly seen to the right, with Blencathra's saddleback outline especially obvious from this angle. Behind you, the Scottish hills look impressive, with Criffel dominating

The high track between Newbiggin and Croglin

the scene. As you reach the top of the first rise, the panorama manages simultaneously to be both beautiful and bleak. ▶

Eventually, soon after passing through the first gate you come to on the track, you reach a junction with another track, along which you bear right. Continue downhill, through a second gate. Turn right at the next junction and then, almost immediately, left to pass a group of buildings on your right. When you reach an asphalt lane, bear right and follow it back into **Croglin**.

Looking to the right over the verdant Eden Valley, a long line of misty Lake District fells fills the horizon, but straight ahead and to the left are the peat moorlands of the Pennines.

THE CROGLIN VAMPIRE

No visit to Croglin would be complete without a retelling of the blood-curdling tale of the Croglin vampire. Depending on which version of the story you hear, the terrifying events happened in either the 19th century or just after the English Civil War and the scene of the vampire attack was either Croglin Low Hall or Croglin Grange.

The owners of the house, the Fishers, had let it to two brothers and a sister, the Cranswells. One balmy summer night the sister was savagely attacked by a mysterious creature that somehow managed to get into ▶

her bedroom and bite her throat. Several months later the creature returned, but this time Miss Cranswell's terrified screams alerted her brothers and they came rushing to her aid with their pistols drawn. One of the brothers shot the creature in the leg and it fled, scrambled over the churchyard wall and disappeared into a vault.

The next day the brothers and several brave villagers went into the vault and discovered that all but one of the coffins had been smashed to pieces. The one that remained intact turned out to contain shrivelled remains with the marks of a recent pistol shot in one leg. They set fire to the coffin and its contents, and the creature was never seen again.

WALK 24
Wetheral to Armathwaite

Distance	8½ miles (13.9km)
Total ascent	378m (1240ft)
Start	Wetheral railway station (NY 467 546)
Finish	Armathwaite railway station (NY 505 463)
Terrain	Riverside paths, fields and quiet lanes
Walking time	4¼ hours
Grade	2
Maps	OS Explorer OL5 and 315 or OS Landranger 86
Transport	Linear route using both the Carlisle–Newcastle and the Settle–Carlisle lines
Refreshments	Eden Coffee Lounge and Crown Hotel, Wetheral; Duke's Head Hotel and Fox and Pheasant Inn, Armathwaite

Making use of two of the many railway lines that radiate out from Carlisle, this linear route links two delightful Eden Valley villages via a long riverside walk. Starting from Wetheral, which is on the Carlisle–Newcastle line, the route passes through an attractive gorge, across pretty meadows and in and out of lovely woodland as it makes its way to Armathwaite. Along the way it visits some mysterious caves cut into the red sandstone cliffs. From Armathwaite walkers can then use the Settle line to return to Carlisle.

If coming from Carlisle, you need to cross the footbridge over the railway when you get off at **Wetheral station**. Head up the access road, towards the village. When you reach the shop, turn left to walk with the village green on your right. The road swings left, heading downhill and past the church. Turn right along the bank of the **River Eden**, through the grass and then up a few steps. The bench beside the river here is another of the Eden Benchmark sculptures. This one is called Flight of Fancy and was created by Tim Shutter.

Map continues on page 146

The large house on the other side of the river is **Corby Castle**. The castle probably started life as a wooden building in the 11th century, and then a stone pele tower was constructed in the 13th century. What you see today, including the classical facade, is mostly 19th century.

Go through a kissing-gate to enter Wetheral Woods, managed by the National Trust. Having climbed gently, the path splits. Bear left to make your way along a narrow path and down some steps to the rock-cut caves known as **St Constantine's Cells**.

143

The steps leading from St Constantine's Cells

St Constantine's Cells are reputed to have been used by either a sixth-century prince or a 10th-century king as a hermitage, although there is no clear evidence to suggest that anyone ever lived in them. It is more likely that they were used as storage chambers by the monks from nearby Wetheral Priory, possibly as a place to hide their valuables during cross-border raids. Wetheral Priory was set up by Benedictine monks in 1106, and was dedicated to the Holy Trinity and St Constantine.

Having visited the caves, retrace your route, back up the steps and then along the narrow path for about 70m until you see some more steps on the left. Climb these to regain the main path, along which you turn left. Do

Wetheral Woods

not be distracted by any paths heading up to the right as you make your way upstream through this lovely wooded gorge.

The next kissing-gate leads into more open country-side. Cross a meadow and then, after a metal gate, climb a track to **Cote House**. When you reach the farm cross the stile beside the large gate. Keep close to the fence on the left and then cross another stile; follow the path down through the trees. As you approach the water's edge pay close attention to the waymarkers, and ensure you walk to the left of the posts.

As you leave the trees and cross a muddy area opposite the south-east end of Cotehouse Island, walk along the rough ground between the river and the fence on your right until you reach the far end of the field. Cross the right-of-way stile on your right – the first stile you will see is a private one – and bear left to cross another one. Now veer right through the trees and past a memorial stone on your left. Bear left at the fork to keep to the riverside path. ▶

The memorial stone was put up by Matthew Knublay, of nearby Cumwhitton, in the mid-19th century in memory of his parents.

145

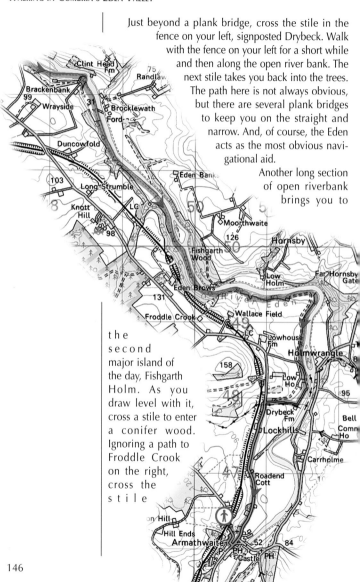

Just beyond a plank bridge, cross the stile in the fence on your left, signposted Drybeck. Walk with the fence on your left for a short while and then along the open river bank. The next stile takes you back into the trees. The path here is not always obvious, but there are several plank bridges to keep you on the straight and narrow. And, of course, the Eden acts as the most obvious navigational aid.

Another long section of open riverbank brings you to the second major island of the day, Fishgarth Holm. As you draw level with it, cross a stile to enter a conifer wood. Ignoring a path to Froddle Crook on the right, cross the stile

The signal station at Armathwaite stands out as a beacon of colour in an otherwise monochrome landscape

Just across the
river you can see
the beautiful red
sandstone that has
been used to build
most of the villages in
the Eden Valley.

directly in front of you to continue close to the water's edge. Just beyond some small rapids, you reach a sign-post close to a tiny shed. Leave the river bank here by turning sharp right, almost heading back on yourself, uphill through the trees. Go through the gate at the top and keep close to the fence on the left.

Having crossed a few stiles and a tiny beck, you will be able to see across the river to some exposed sandstone cliffs. You now need to cross the hidden stile in the fence corner and then turn left to head straight down the steep embankment. At the bottom, turn right to resume the riverside route. A kissing-gate eventually gives you access to the riverbank proper. ◀

Continuing upstream, bear left along a rough track which eventually reaches **Drybeck Farm**. Now follow the lane round to the right. Turn left at the T-junction near a viaduct and walk along the road into **Armathwaite**. Soon after the village shop, take the road turning on the right and follow this uphill. To return to Carlisle, ignore the first pedestrian access to the station and continue under the railway bridge. The station entrance is then about 100m on the right.

WALK 25

Talkin Fell and Simmerson Hill

Distance	6¼ miles (10.1km)
Total ascent	390m (1280ft)
Start/finish	Blacksmiths Arms, Talkin (NY 549 573). Please park considerately nearby in the village
Terrain	Good tracks, quiet lanes and open moorland, wet in places
Walking time	3¾ hrs
Grade	2–3
Maps	OS Explorer 315 or OS Landranger 86
Transport	Talkin is served by bus 97
Refreshments	Blacksmiths Arms, Talkin

They say good things come in small packages and that seems particularly apt for this walk onto two very low-lying tops in the Pennines. After a fairly gentle climb from Talkin village, you reach one of the best viewpoints in this part of Cumbria. Topped by a collection of tall cairns and a trig pillar, Talkin Fell (1250ft) is a wonderful place to stand at the end of a sunny spring afternoon, admiring the views and listening to the curlews returning to their nesting sites. The route then crosses to nearby Simmerson Hill (1312ft) before dropping into Geltsdale, one of the loveliest and loneliest of Pennine valleys.

Stand facing the Blacksmiths Arms in **Talkin** village and take the quiet road to the left of the pub, towards Forest Head. After about 500m take the road turning on your right. The road swings sharp left and then comes to an abrupt end just after the buildings at **Talkin Head**. ▶

Continue straight ahead on the rough track, climbing steadily. As you reach an area of woodland to the right of the track, you catch your first glimpse of the tall cairns on top of Talkin Fell. You also pass a signposted bridleway to the right of the track. Ignore it at this stage, but this will form part of your return route later in the day. Surprisingly quickly, your surroundings take on a much wilder nature as you look up into Geltsdale.

Talkin comes from the Celtic word *talcan* meaning 'brow of the hill'.

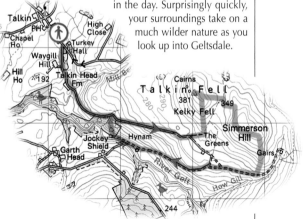

GELTSDALE

Geltsdale is part of a 5,400-hectare nature reserve run by the RSPB. It is one of the few sites in England where the rare hen harrier can still be found. Other breeding birds include merlin, golden plover, ring ouzel, curlew, lapwing, redshank and snipe. More than 300 species of flowering plants have been recorded, including national rarities such as pale forget-me-not and spring sandwort.

There is even a chance of seeing the beautiful, but increasingly rare black grouse – if you're extremely lucky. These birds have suffered a devastating decline in numbers in England over the last hundred years or so, mostly due to over-grazing and loss of habitat. They are now confined to the North Pennines and parts of Northumberland and North Yorkshire.

Visit soon after daybreak in spring and you might catch sight of the male birds 'lekking'. The lek is the birds' famous flamboyant display, which the females attend to choose a mate. In this impressive dance the males spread their tail feathers, showing off their magnificent glossy black plumage, extend their wings and inflate the distinctive red 'combs' above each eye. They crouch and circle the ground and spar with each other in a bid to dominate the site and become the females' choice of mate.

The track onto the fell follows the line of a drystone wall for much of the way

The summit of Talkin Fell

Eventually you lose the fence/wall on your right. About 250m after going through a gate to the left of a sheepfold, the wall on your left swings left. You soon reach a fork; bear right here, away from the wall. Step across the wooden gate in the fence and then continue in the same direction for just a few more metres, across a boggy area, and then turn left to head up the fellside on a narrow path.

When you reach the wall you are joined by another faint trail coming in from the left and the two now make their way to a ladder stile. Cross this and you will see the trig pillar of **Talkin Fell** straight ahead. ▶ From the summit retrace your steps, across the ladder stile and down the peaty path, remembering to fork left when the path splits. When you reach the bottom of the slope, do not re-cross the wooden gate; instead, keep straight ahead, walking parallel with the fence on your right. Go through the metal gate in the fence and then turn left along a narrow path to the right of the fence.

Just beyond the summit trig pillar the decidedly eerie tall cairns stand guard along the western edge of the fell.

151

Climb the small jumble of rocks forming a rim around the entire western edge of **Simmerson Hill** and turn right along a path following the edge of this heathery fell. On reaching a fence, bear right to head downhill. The track is less obvious now, but it follows the line of the fence down to a much wider, clearer track, along which you turn right.

The old mine workers' cottages at **Gairs** may just be discernible in the valley below as you descend from Simmerson Hill. The Gairs mine formed part of the East Cumberland Coalfield, which is thought to be one of the oldest in England, possibly even worked by the Romans. At its peak in the 1920s, almost 200 men worked at Gairs, producing around 70,000 tons of coal per year. It was abandoned in 1936. The mine's rail line, which forms part of one of the earliest industrial railways in the world, ran to nearby Hallbankgate.

After about 500m keep left at a fork in the track. Far below, the noisy River Gelt rushes through the wooded valley. You soon join a path coming down from the right and, before you know it, the track drops to the edge of the **River Gelt** near some buildings. Continue along the clear track on the northern side of the river. The gorge here is particularly spectacular, as a huge volume of water tries to make its way through the narrowest of gaps.

When you reach the gate leading on to private land at **Low Hynam**, bear right to head along a gated track that climbs steadily through the woods to emerge on to the track that you followed earlier in the walk. Turn left along it and retrace your steps to **Talkin**.

WALK 26

Talkin Tarn and the Gelt

Distance	7¾ miles (12.6km)
Total ascent	348m (1142ft)
Start/finish	Talkin Tarn car park (NY 543 590)
Terrain	Farm paths, woodland, tracks and quiet lanes
Walking time	4½ hrs
Grade	2
Maps	OS Explorer 315 or OS Landranger 86
Transport	Talkin is served by bus 97; the route also passes close to Brampton railway station, which is on the Carlisle–Newcastle line
Refreshments	Blacksmiths Arms, Talkin; Boathouse Tea Room at Talkin Tarn

'If local people eat there, it's likely to be a good restaurant', so tourists are told wherever they travel. And, if Talkin Tarn and Gelt Woods are anything to go by, the same is true for beauty spots. On warm summer Sundays the car park at Talkin Tarn gets very busy as the population of the surrounding towns and villages descends on this attractive body of water; while the paths through the woods are full of dog-walkers and families out for a stroll.

The best times to visit are the beginning and end of the day when the light on the tarn is simply magical, and photographers line up with their tripods to capture the mood. Autumn colours seem particularly vibrant in the fascinating gorge cut by the often tumultuous River Gelt, and this is also a good time of year to spot red squirrels stocking up on food for the winter.

From the main pay-and-display car park, head down to Talkin Tarn and turn left to begin walking along the path beside the water. You soon pass the boathouse, which is home to a tearoom and public toilets, as well as one of the oldest non-collegiate rowing clubs in the country.

153

An evening stroll around Talkin Tarn

Talkin Tarn, fed by underground streams, is glacial in origin. It is a kettle-hole lake, formed when a block of ice broke away from the main glacier and was left stranded in the sandy deposits left by the meltwater. When the ice-block eventually melted, it left a depression filled with water.

Talkin Tarn Amateur Rowing Club celebrated its 150th birthday in 2009, making it the second oldest rowing club in the north of England after the Tyne Rowing Club. Races were first held on the tarn in the 1850s. Over the years the club's members have competed in the Olympic Games, international regattas, the World Rowing Championships and World Masters Rowing Championships in various countries.

Beyond the trees the tarn-side path swings right. Leave it here by turning left, towards a kissing-gate in the field corner. The path negotiates a wet area via stone slabs before continuing up the meadow to another gate. Beyond this the path skirts some woodland and works

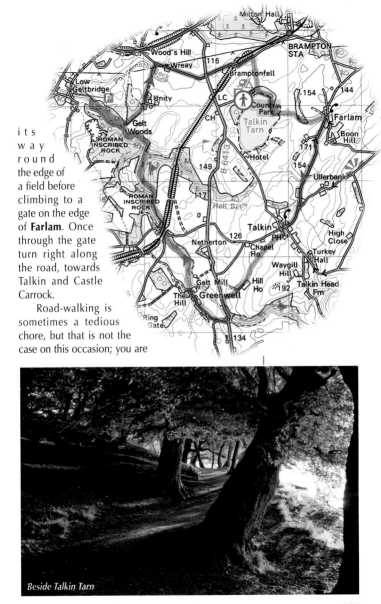

its way round the edge of a field before climbing to a gate on the edge of **Farlam**. Once through the gate turn right along the road, towards Talkin and Castle Carrock.

Road-walking is sometimes a tedious chore, but that is not the case on this occasion; you are

Beside Talkin Tarn

unlikely to encounter much traffic. You will have plenty of opportunity along the road to enjoy the views across to the tarn on your right and, as the road climbs, ahead towards the Lake District.

When you reach **Talkin** village, pass a road turning on your left. Immediately after the tiny 'green' in front of the Blacksmiths Arms turn left along a gravel track. As you enter the parking area at the side of the pub, you will see a well-hidden set of steps in the wall corner on your right. This marks the start of the next section of footpath. Once over the wall, follow the narrow trail through the trees, cross a private driveway and then climb the stile in the fence. Now make for the small gate on the other side of this paddock and then continue in the same direction through the next field. Go through the metal gate and walk with the fence on your right until you join a clear track.

This takes you up towards **Hill House**. Follow the waymarkers through the yard, in front of the ornate Victorian farmhouse and then on to a lane. When the lane swings sharp right, bear left on to a grassy track between a hedge and a wall. At the end of this, go through the gate immediately in front of you, bear half-right and drop to stile beside a gate.

The pub at Talkin bathed in late evening sunshine

Turn left along the road and follow it as it drops to a bridge over the **River Gelt**. You then climb slightly and, 100m beyond the bridge, turn right along a wide track. Follow this as it crosses a stream and goes through a pair of green metal gates. Keep right at Greenwell Meadows as the path descends to a gravel courtyard in front of a row of delightfully isolated cottages at **Greenwell**. Now keep straight ahead, through another gate and on to a surfaced lane.

Early autumn in Gelt Woods

The hamlet of **Greenwell** is home to Gelt Mill, which was built in 1776. Until the end of the 19th century it took water from the Gelt via a series of sluice gates, but the works were destroyed by a flood in 1894. After this it was driven by water from Castle Carrock Beck. The mill was closed in 1939 and then converted into a private home in the 1980s. The mill pond, sluice gates, shafts and cog wheels have all been restored.

A skeleton in full battle gear was once found in a tree near this pretty hamlet. It is thought he had been fleeing from the bloody battle between followers of Mary Queen of Scots and royal cavalrymen in

1570. The three-day clash, sometimes known as the Battle of Gelt Bridge, resulted in the slaughter of many hundreds of men, with the superior rebel forces being beaten. This was just one of many skirmishes involving northern Catholic noblemen seeking to depose Queen Elizabeth I and replace her with her cousin Mary.

The woodland, with alder and ash on the lower slopes and birch and oak higher up, is home to red squirrels, roe deer and a variety of birdlife including kingfishers, woodpeckers, chiffchaffs and dippers.

Walk along the asphalt until the lane bends left just after the final building on your right. Leave it here by crossing the stile beside the gate on your right. You now follow a peaceful stretch of river for just over 800m, crossing several fields.

When you reach the road near the impressive **Gelt Bridge Viaduct**, completed in 1835, turn right to pass under the arch and then right again at the junction. Immediately after crossing the road bridge over the river, turn left through the gate into **Gelt Woods** and walk through the beautiful, wooded gorge with the rushing River Gelt on your left and tall red sandstone cliffs on either side. ◄

There are at least a couple of paths off into the woods on your right, but ignore them and keep to the path nearest the river for 2.25km. After a fork, you will cross a 'causeway' at the base of low cliffs.

High above the causeway is the Roman **Written Rock of Gelt**. Dating back to AD207, it records the quarry workings of Roman soldiers belonging to the Second Legion. Tennyson wrote of the rock: 'The Vexillary hath left crag-carven o'er the streaming Gelt' in his *Idylls of the King*. Sadly, the steps that once led to the rock high above the main path have been badly eroded and the route up to it is dangerous.

The river here forces itself through an unusual winding channel through the smooth bedrock and then makes a sharp bend to the right. (The curious potholes in the opposite bank of the river at the bend have been formed over thousands of years as stones, spinning in the fast-moving water, have eroded the sandstone bedrock.) Soon after it does so, the path climbs to a wooden bench. Leave the river by turning sharp right, almost back on yourself on a clear, wide path that runs parallel with the path you were just following, but at a higher point in the woods.

On reaching a junction of paths near a fence, turn left. When the wide, muddy path splits, bear right, through a metal kissing-gate. Follow the wall on your right until you reach a farm building at **Unity**. Just after this the path swings right, through a gate to join a lane. Turn left and then right at the end of the lane.

Go straight over the road and continue along the surfaced lane. Soon after crossing the railway bridge, the road rises and then dips. As it starts to head downhill, go through the gate on the right. Follow the vehicle track, but when this disintegrates into nothing more than muddy ruts, keep to the fence on your right.

Beyond the next kissing-gate continue in the same direction on a vague path through the trees. When you reach the tarn turn right to return to retrace your steps to **Talkin Tarn** car park.

WALK 27
Quarry Beck and Ridgewood

Distance	4 miles (6.4km)
Total ascent	114m (375ft)
Start/finish	Parking and picnic area on the north side of Lanercost Bridge over the River Irthing (NY 553 633). If approaching from the south, watch for a gap in the hedges on your left just over the bridge, giving access to the parking area.
Terrain	Woodland paths, tracks and country roads
Walking time	2hrs
Grade	1–2
Maps	OS Explorer 315 or OS Landranger 86
Transport	Lanercost is served by the Hadrian's Wall Bus AD122, April to October only. Brampton is served by buses 94, 95 and 680
Refreshments	Lanercost Tearooms

Beautiful Quarry Beck is hidden away in a peaceful wooded valley just to the south of Lanercost, while Ridgewood is a line of high ground with surprisingly good views over the surrounding countryside. Linking the two via quiet country roads, this walk forms a gentle stroll. Bluebells add to the pleasure in May.

Starting from the parking and picnic area beside the pretty **River Irthing**, cross the old **Lanercost Bridge**. The old bridge was built in 1724 to replace earlier bridges that were destroyed by floods. Traffic stopped using it in 1962 when the less attractive road bridge was built next to it. On reaching Abbey Bridge house, still sometimes mistaken for the inn that it once was, turn right along the road. After about 140m carefully cross over and turn left along a footpath signposted 'Easby Lane End via Quarry Beck'.

Dropping into the peaceful, secluded gorge, you pass waterfalls, small meadows and occasional outcrops of gorgeous red sandstone as you follow the beck upstream. The peace is temporarily broken as you cross the road leading into the stoneworks, but the sound of drills and sawing is quickly replaced by more soothing birdsong and the gentle bubbling of the beck on its way to the River Irthing.

You sadly part company with the beck as you draw level with some homes on the other side of the water. The path now heads up

The bluebell woods of Quarry Beck

through the trees to reach the road, along which you turn left. Be careful here because there is no path and the road is winding with high hedges. Things soon get better as you pick up a path running alongside the road all the way into **Brampton**.

Just 120m after passing a turning to the left at the edge of the green on the outskirts of the town, turn right up a broad but rough track, signposted 'The Ridge'. At the top of the rise, bear right to pass in front of some cottages. Go through an old metal kissing-gate and then follow a line of beautiful beech trees along the crest of the low ridge. ◄ You have the Pennines over to the right, but it's the panorama to the left that really catches the eye, backed by the Scottish hills.

Walk with the fence on your right at first, but then pass through another metal kissing-gate to continue with the field boundary on your left. The route rises gently before dipping to a squeeze stile beside a gate. Beyond this keep straight ahead, ignoring the track to the right.

You are less than 150m above sea level here and yet the views are wonderful.

The view from Ridgewood

As you pass through denser woodland, stick to the wide, mostly level path – do not be tempted by paths heading off into the trees.

Massive beech trees in Ridgewood

You finally leave the ridge 30m after first encountering a wire fence on your right at a break in the trees. Now, as indicated by the waymarker on a fencepost, bear left down a narrow path that weaves its way through the stunted woodland. Going through the metal kissing-gate at the bottom of this path, turn right, go through another gate in a few metres and you will eventually find yourself at the roadside. Turn left and then right, and then left to rejoin the main road. It is now an easy stroll back to **Lanercost Bridge**.

LANCERCOST PRIORY

For a short but worth-while detour, continue just 500m along the road to visit atmospheric Lancercost Priory. This was founded by Augustinian canons in 1166. Being so close to the Scottish border, it has had a turbulent history. The priory suffered its first raid in 1280 following a visit by Edward I, ▶

but the most damaging attack came in 1346 when King David II of Scotland ransacked the monastic buildings, desecrated the priory church and wasted lands belonging to the priory.

Lanercost's unusual claim to fame is that for five months in 1306–7 a dying Edward I ruled his kingdom from here, having summoned Parliament to Carlisle and moved the seals of the crown to Lanercost, effectively making it the capital.

During the Dissolution of the Monasteries in 1536, the site was granted to Sir Thomas Dacre who converted the west range buildings into a private residence. In the middle of the 19th century the ruins of the nave were restored and turned into an attractive parish church by the renowned architect Anthony Salvin. The substantial remains of the north and south transepts, the choir, the sanctuary and the cellarium are now in the care of English Heritage, and are open to the public from April to October; there is an admission fee.

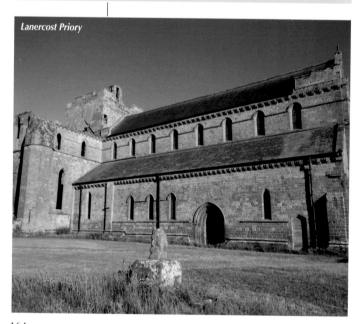

Lanercost Priory

WALK 28

Carlisle to Rockcliffe along the River Eden

Distance	8 miles (12.9km)
Total ascent	180m (590ft)
Start	Bitts Park pay and display car park, Carlisle (NY 398 563)
Finish	Bus shelter in front of Rockcliffe Primary School (NY 359 618)
Terrain	City parks, pavement, riverside paths
Walking time	4¼ hrs
Grade	1–2
Maps	OS Explorer 315 or OS Landranger 85
Transport	There is a wide variety of transport options for getting to and from Carlisle, including several train lines. To return to the city from Rockcliffe at the end of the walk, catch bus 101
Refreshments	Crown and Thistle Inn, Rockcliffe; good selection of pubs, cafés and restaurants in Carlisle

By the time the River Eden reaches the historic city of Carlisle, it is entering the final stages of its meandering journey to the sea. While families stroll in the parks bordering it and kayakers mess around on the weir, otters play on the muddy banks and kingfishers flash by at great speed. A path hugs the river's edge almost all the way from the city to the village of Rockcliffe, providing lots of opportunities to spot some of the wildlife. There is plenty of history too along the way, from the Romans to cross-border smugglers.

CARLISLE

Carlisle's original motte and bailey castle was built by William Rufus in 1092 on the site of a Roman fortress. The oldest surviving part of Carlisle Castle today is the keep, begun in the 12th century by Henry I of England and completed by David I of Scotland, a good illustration of how control over the border city was constantly changing hands.

The city itself has been an important administrative centre for nearly two millennia, since the Romans established Luguvalium here and then built Hadrian's Wall, which crossed the River Eden at Carlisle. In the ▶

troubled centuries that followed Roman rule, control of the city passed from Celts to Anglians to Scots to English to Scots to English to Scots to English... Carlisle's history from at least the 11th century onwards is the history of England's border with Scotland, a troubled and very often bloody history. No other English city has endured so many assaults on it, and the castle was held by the Scots as recently as 1745 when Bonnie Prince Charlie marched into Carlisle and proclaimed his father King James VIII of Scotland and James III of England.

Carlisle Castle is owned by English Heritage and is open to the public daily, except at Christmas and New Year. There is an admission charge.

There has been a bridge across the Eden in Carlisle since at least Roman times, but this one was built in 1815 and widened in the early 1930s.

Heading away from the walls of **Carlisle Castle**, leave the car park and walk into Bitts Park. Keeping straight ahead at a crossing of paths, you will soon see the **River Eden** on your left. Use the pedestrian tunnel to walk under the road bridge and then turn right. At the top of the slope, turn right along the pavement and go over the bridge. ◄ Having crossed the river, turn right through the gap in

Carlisle Castle

the bridge wall. Veer right at the bottom of the steps to skirt the edge of the ornamental garden. Immediately after a gate, look to your right and you will see a number of grassy paths heading down the embankment towards the river. Take the right-hand option, which passes to the right of a solitary horse chestnut tree and goes through a kissing-gate under one of the bridge arches.

The path soon passes around the edge of the Edenside cricket ground. As you reach an area of picnic tables, you will see the River Caldew entering the Eden from the south.

The 30-mile long **River Caldew** is one of the Eden's main tributaries. It rises on the eastern slopes of Skiddaw, England's fourth highest mountain. At one time, its banks were home to many textile mills, employing hundreds of people. The first textile factory opened in Carlisle in 1724, but it was not until the laws on the use of cotton were relaxed in 1774 that the industry really took off. By the 1840s the Caldew had helped to turn the city and its surrounding villages into

Map continues on page 169

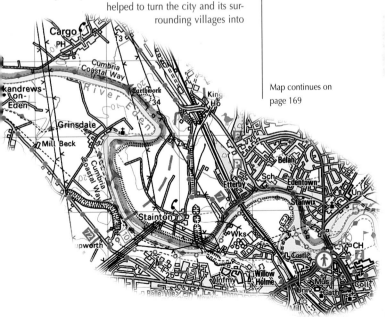

The bridge carrying the old Waverley Route

The Waverley Route from Carlisle to Edinburgh, opened in 1862 and closed in 1969, was named after Sir Walter Scott's 'Waverley' novels, which were set in the border area.

the fourth most important textile-producing area in the country.

Turn left on reaching a surfaced walkway past a row of homes and up to the road. Continue along the pavement in the same direction, heading gently uphill. Take the first road turning on the left, Etterby Road, and follow it for 500m, crossing the railway as you go.

When the road swings round to the right to become Stainton Road leave it by taking the track to the left of the bend, to re-emerge on the river bank where the path splits. Keep left to stay on top of the embankment. When you reach the old Waverley Route bridge, head down to the left to go under one of the arches and through a kissing-gate. ◀

The path is faint on the ground here as it crosses farmland; simply keep close to the river and you shouldn't go wrong. At the time of writing, a new road bridge was being built over the Eden here. The path will eventually go under the fly-over, but walkers may face lengthy diversions well into 2011.

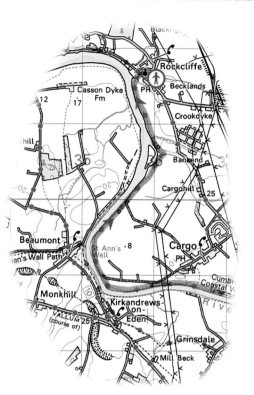

As you draw level with **Grinsdale** on the opposite side, the public right-of-way keeps to the river bank; do not be tempted to cut the corner as the river performs a sharp bend to the right. Only when you reach a gully cutting across your path will you have to deviate away from the river for a few metres to find a convenient place to cross.

Continue downstream, cross a stile in a fence and turn left along the edge of the field. Cross a wooden step stile and keep close to the fence on the left as you climb the steep slope ahead. At the top cross the stile and bear left, continuing with the fence on your left. The river is

169

The River Eden near Grinsdale

now some distance below. As you reach the crest of the hill, you can see the hills of southern Scotland in the distance.

Always with the fence on your left, cross several more stiles and then drop down to a narrow footbridge. Having crossed, bear left to regain the water's edge. Ignore all the paths off to the right; simply keep to the river bank.

Soon you will see the buildings of **Beaumont** just ahead and on the other side of the river. The river swings right now. Keep steadfastly to the bank, eventually passing the ruins of the 'fish house' at King Garth.

SALMON IN THE RIVER EDEN

The River Eden used to be one of the most important salmon fisheries in the country. In fact, many of the largest salmon ever caught in England were caught in these waters. The king granted part of the fishery to the city of Carlisle in the 12th century. The 'fish house' was built in 1733 to house bailiffs and boats. Mayoral dinners were also held here until 1892 when the fishery was abandoned.

In December and January Atlantic salmon swim from the sea to the higher reaches of the Eden, sometimes as far upstream as Stenkrith at Kirkby Stephen, to spawn. The female lays her eggs on the bottom of shallow rivers and streams, covering them with gravel after they have been fertilised by the male. The young hatch in April and May, and spend the first six years of their lives in the river. They eventually migrate to the sea and remain there for up to three years, returning to spawn in the area of the river where they were born.

Although stocks have declined due to a combination of over-fishing at sea and pollution, the Eden is still a fine salmon river and remains one of the cleanest in England.

One of the more unusual methods used to catch both salmon and trout is known as haaf-netting. This ancient method of fishing is said to date back to the Norsemen and is still practised in the waters of the Solway Firth. Only a small but hardy and determined group of fishermen – there are about 50 left in Cumbria – continue to use the 'haaf net' (meaning 'sea net'). Like a giant butterfly net, it is mounted on a frame about 6m wide and 1.5m high and supported by three legs. The fishermen heave these cumbersome contraptions on to their shoulders, tramp out over the gloopy mudflats and stand waist-deep ▶

in the cold water waiting for the fish to come along. They hold the central 'leg' as the net is placed across the current. The net then streams out in the water and, when fish swim into it, the other two legs of the frame are allowed to float to the surface. This traps the fish, which are then dispatched by a blow from a mallet, known as a 'nep'.

Just after passing a public byroad to **Cargo**, with Rockcliffe in sight now, the path enters an area of commons known as Carr Bed. There are three channels feeding into the Eden here, all of which are crossed via footbridges that you will find a little way back from the river itself. There is a faint winding path linking them all.

Beyond the last of the three bridges, the only one with proper railings on both sides, the path veers left to return to the river bank. Cross another bridge as you draw level with the northern tip of a small grassy island in the

Cattle go down to the River Eden to drink

river. Bear right at the waymarker, over the stile, and turn left to walk with the fence on your left.

After passing Rockcliffe's cricket pitch, bear half-right to cross to a gate. Beyond this, turn right to cross a footbridge. Turn right along the lane beside the church and then left at the road. ▶

Follow the road round to the left, towards Rockcliffe Cross and Floriston. The bus shelter, located in front of **Rockcliffe Primary School**, is a few metres ahead on the right. ▶

St Mary's churchyard contains the remains of a thousand-year-old Norse cross.

For more information about Rockcliffe's past see Walk 30.

WALK 29
Burgh Marsh

Distance	7 miles (11.3km)
Total ascent	99m (325ft)
Start/finish	St Michael's Church, Burgh by Sands (NY 328 591)
Terrain	Quiet lanes, open marsh, muddy riverbank, farm paths
Walking time	3hrs
Grade	1–2
Maps	OS Explorer 315 or OS Landranger 85
Transport	Burgh by Sands is served by bus 93, and from April to October by the Hadrian's Wall Bus AD122
Refreshments	Greyhound Inn, Burgh by Sands

As long as you check the tide tables and weather conditions before setting out and don't stray too far from established routes, the Solway salt-marshes can be a fascinating and beautiful area to explore. Steeped in the dark often bloody tales associated with border history, Burgh Marsh stretches for several miles to the west of Carlisle. Stand at the spot where King Edward I died while waiting to take his army across the ford into Scotland, and the grassy flatlands seem to go on forever. Somewhere out there is the channel of the River Eden, inching its way ever closer to its rendezvous with Scotland's River Esk to flow together into the Solway Firth. ▶

After crossing the marsh, the route follows the Eden upstream for a few miles, past Rockcliffe on the opposite bank, finally leaving the river at the hidden hamlet of Beaumont. From here the border theme is picked up again as you follow the Hadrian's Wall Path back to Burgh.

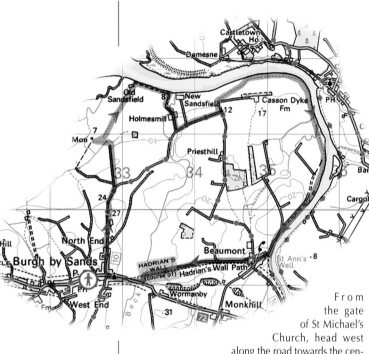

From the gate of St Michael's Church, head west along the road towards the centre of **Burgh by Sands**. ◄ After 140m, before reaching the main part of the village, turn right along a narrow lane.

The statue of King Edward I on Burgh's village green was unveiled by the Duke of Kent in 2007 to commemorate the 700th anniversary of Edward's death.

Burgh by Sands is home to some unusual architecture. There is a thatched cottage on the right, rare in Cumbria, as you head out of the village, but more unusual are the clay dabbins. These are homes with walls built from a mixture of clay, stones and straw. It is a method of construction that probably dates back to the 15th century.

After about 1.3km, at a right-hand bend in the lane, turn left along a track. Bear right at the fork and follow the track until it bends sharp right. Climb the stile next to the gate here and then cross the next field. Two stiles and a bridge follow in quick succession to reach the marsh proper. Make your way over to the fenced monument.

The **Edward I Monument** was built in 1685 to mark the site where the king died on 7 July 1307. Edward had been at war with the Scots since 1295, leading his army into battle on several occasions – hence his nickname 'Hammer of the Scots'. He died of dysentery while camped here on the marsh, close to the place where his army was hoping to cross the River Eden at low tide to enter Scotland. His body was later taken to St Michael's Church in the village to lie in state before being taken back to London.

The Edward I Monument complete with Scottish graffiti

This old farmhouse was once an inn frequented by those trading with Scotland across the ford, or wath. It appears in Sir Walter Scott's *Red Gauntlet* as the inn called the Lady Lowther.

From the monument head back towards the fence you crossed earlier, and follow the line of this field boundary north-east across the access land until you reach **Old Sandsfield** and the **River Eden**. ◄

Go through the kissing-gate in the fence and then follow the Cumbria Coastal Way along the muddy embankment in front of the farmhouse. Later follow a track away from the river, over a bridge and between the buildings at **Holmesmill**. Turn left at the T-junction and then left again when the lane bends right. As this too swings right, go through the kissing-gate and bear right along the indistinct path to Beaumont. A series of yellow waymarkers and two wooden bridges guide you to a stile at the river's edge. Once over this head right upstream.

As it flows into the Solway Firth the **River Eden** plays host to one of the UK's few tidal bores. These occur when the leading edge of the incoming tide forms a wave as it is funnelled into a shallow narrowing river via a broad bay. In some conditions the tidal bore on the Eden reaches a height of about a metre and travels

Looking down the Eden towards Old Sandsfield

Rockcliffe

at seven knots. At these times the wave is clearly visible and the sudden rush of the water can be heard from quite some distance.

▶ As you draw level with **Rockcliffe** on the opposite bank, the strip of land between the fence on the right and the Eden on the left narrows until you cross a stile and continue with the fence on your left. The path recrosses the fence in a short while, but quickly crosses back again.

After having crossed two bridges, bear right, away from the water's edge, for the next stile. Now continue parallel with the river and cross a steep-sided channel via a bridge. Swing right to pick up a vague track through the grass. This becomes clearer and, as it does so, leave it by bearing left along the riverbank. On encountering another deep channel, swing right to cross it via a bridge.

Continue alongside the River Eden and, eventually, you will reach a steep wooded slope on your right. After a stile the path is very overgrown in places. Climb some steps up to the right and go through a gate. Turn left along the lane and follow it into **Beaumont**.

Rockcliffe is named after the red sandstone cliffs that you see just to the west of the village. It is from the old Norse *rauǒr* (red) and the old English *clif* (cliff).

Turn right at the church and then left along a narrow lane. You are now following the **Hadrian's Wall Path**, which runs for 84 miles from Wallsend on Tyneside to Bowness-on-Solway.

HADRIAN'S WALL

Hadrian's Wall was constructed under the orders of the Emperor Hadrian after his visit to Britain in AD122. He wanted, according to his biographer, to 'separate the Romans from the barbarians'. Over the next six years professional soldiers, or legionaries, built a wall about 5m high and 80 Roman miles long (73 modern miles) from Wallsend on the River Tyne in the east to Bowness-on-Solway in Cumbria in the west. Today, it is a UNESCO World Heritage Site.

Little evidence remains of the wall west of Carlisle, although there are signs, as you leave the track and head towards Burgh on the Hadrian's Wall Path, of the Vallum – the high-sided defensive ditch the Romans built parallel to the wall. Watch for it after the sign requesting people to refrain from walking in single file. There would also have been a major fort at Burgh, known as Aballava, plus several marching camps around the Grinsdale and Beaumont area. The soldiers were based here to guard the waths.

Do not be tempted by any turnings; simply keep straight ahead on this track. After narrowing and passing through a gate, the route keeps to the left of a line of trees where you are requested not to walk in single file to help protect the archaeology. Yellow waymarkers guide you across a gated bridge, beyond which you bear left and follow the hedges on your right to the road. Turn right and then, just after a layby, go through the kissing-gate to the right of the road to pick up the continuation of the Hadrian's Wall Path. Keep close to the hedge on your left and then, after the next gate, turn right along the road to return to St Michael's Church in **Burgh by Sands**.

WALK 30
Rockcliffe Marsh

Distance	7½ miles (12.1km)
Total ascent	76m (250ft)
Start/finish	St Mary's Church, Rockcliffe (NY 359 617). Please park considerately nearby in the village
Terrain	Riverbank, marshland, farm paths, roads
Walking time	3¼ hours
Grade	1–2
Maps	OS Explorer 315 or OS Landranger 85
Transport	Rockcliffe is served by bus 101
Refreshments	Crown and Thistle Inn, Rockcliffe

With the now brackish waters of the River Eden lapping up against the edge of immense salt-marshes, this route gives walkers a sense of the Solway's wide open spaces as well as a glimpse of the Scottish hills in the distance. Huge flocks of birds gather here in the autumn and, come the spring, wild flowers bring vivid bursts of colour to the marsh. We also stray for the first time out of the Eden catchment and up to the River Esk at Metalbridge, just a stone's throw from the border.

Head down the lane to the left of St Mary's Church in **Rockcliffe** and follow it across a small bridge. ▶ The lane soon gains a little height, providing snatched glimpses of

The last of the 10 Eden Benchmarks, a sculpture by Anthony Turner called 'Global Warming' (pictured), is in the open area on your left.

both the northern Lake District fells to the left and the final few miles of the River Eden as it widens and flows into the Solway Firth. As the lane bends sharp right, take the signposted footpath to the left, towards Demesne Marsh. Cross the stile at the bottom of the slope and follow the path along the river bank.

Castletown House, up to the right, was built at the beginning of the 19th century by Robert Mounsey, a forebear of the current occupiers. During World War I it served as an auxiliary hospital for troops injured on the western front.

Soon after passing **Demesne**, the white house up to the right, cross a deep steep-sided channel. There is no bridge here, so you may have to head a few metres upstream to leap across. Cross a stile next to a gate; remember this place because you will return to it after your stroll out on to the marsh. Continue along the river bank, until you draw level with an isolated farmhouse on the other side of the

180

channel. This is **Old Sandsfield** (see Walk 29 for information).

Looking across the Eden to Old Sandsfield

Rockcliffe Marsh, one of the largest salt-marshes in Cumbria, stretches on into the distance ahead. This forms part of the Solway Coast Area of Outstanding Natural Beauty, designated in 1964 and stretching all the way from Rockcliffe to Maryport.

Sadly, there is no public access beyond this point, so you now need to retrace your steps to the stile beside the gate you crossed earlier. Recross it and turn left beside the fence. Cross the stile at the top of the short slope and then turn right along the rough track. Follow this as it swings left near **Demesne**, and then when it swings right go through the small gate on your left. Keep close to the hedge on your left and then leave the tiny paddock via a stile. Continue in the same direction on a rough lane, ignoring a track to the left when the lane swings right at **Croftends**.

Turn left at the T-junction and walk along the road for about 110m. Just after passing **Croftends Farm** on the left, turn right over a stile. Keep the hedgerow on your left for about 200m, until you reach a stile in the fence on your left. Cross this and then continue with a fence on your right. Follow this as it turns left. You then cross the next stile on your right. Turn right to walk along the edge of the field.

St Mary's Church, Rockcliffe

Turn left along the road and, immediately after passing the farmhouse at **Halltown**, turn right along a rough track. Just as the track heads into the yard, cross the stile next to the gate on the left. The next stile is a little hard to spot, but you should continue in roughly the same direction (ENE). Once over the stile and the small bridge, the path swings half-left through the trees, soon picking up a sparse line of hedgerow and crossing another stile. Continue between the hedge on your left and a low wire fence on your right for a short while before picking up a wide grassy track, muddy in places.

As you near the farm at **Garriestown**, watch for a stile up to your right. Once over this, keep the fence on your left, following it round to the left. Go through the gate and turn right along the farm track. Turn left at the junction and then cross the railway over the footbridge.

Once over the stile on the other side keep close to the hedges on your right. As you approach the bridge carrying the **M6** over the **River Esk**, turn right to cross a stile. Walk with the fence on your left and follow it when it swings left. Go through the gate and follow the lane to a road. Turn right and you soon reach a T-junction next to the motorway.

As you turn right, towards Carlisle, you begin nearly 4km of road walking to return to Rockcliffe. Apart from the first brief and very noisy section beside the M6, most of it is on quiet country roads. Turn right at the next T-junction to follow the road all the way back to Rockcliffe. It goes over a level crossing and makes a couple of left-hand bends. When it finally enters the village, follow it round to the right to return to the church in **Rockcliffe**.

A pleasantly sleepy little village now, **Rockcliffe** has a colourful past. In the 18th century it was a commercial port and ship-building centre. Later it became an important staging post along the route used to smuggle whisky and brandy from Scotland to England. Due to differential duties on spirits, alcohol bought north of the border could be sold for five times as much in England. Several excise men were based in the village, but many Rockcliffe homes were storehouses for smuggled whisky.

APPENDIX A

Route summary table

Walk no	Start	Finish	Distance	Time	Grade	Page
1	Garsdale station	Kirkby Stephen station	17 miles (27.2km)	9hrs	5	28
2	Garsdale station	Kirkby Stephen station	12 miles (19.3km)	7hrs	5	36
3	Kirkby Stephen	Kirkby Stephen	9 miles (14.3km)	4½ hrs	2	41
4	Kirkby Stephen station	Appleby station	15 miles (24.2km)	6½ hrs	3	46
5	Near Newbiggin-on-Lune	Near Newbiggin-on-Lune	8½ miles (13.7km)	4¼hrs	2–3	54
6	Near Orton	Near Orton	8½ miles (13.7km)	4hrs	2–3	58
7	Crosby Ravensworth	Crosby Ravensworth	6½ miles (10.5km)	3½hrs	2–3	62
8	Maulds Meaburn	Maulds Meaburn	5 miles (8km)	2½hrs	2	67
9	Hoff	Hoff	5 miles (8km)	2½hrs	1–2	71
10	King's Meaburn	King's Meaburn	6¼ miles (10km)	3hrs	2	75
11	Bampton Grange	Bampton Grange	5 miles (8km)	2hrs	1	80
12	Askham	Askham	7¼ miles (11.8km)	3hrs	1–2	84
13	Dufton	Dufton	8¾ miles (14km)	4½hrs	2	90
14	Dufton	Dufton	4 miles (6.6km)	3hrs	3	95
15	Dufton	Dufton	10 miles (16km)	5½hrs	4	98

Walk no	Start	Finish	Distance	Time	Grade	Page
16	Near Eamont Bridge	Near Eamont Bridge	3¾ miles (6.1km)	1¾hrs	1	103
17	Culgaith	Culgaith	6¾ miles (11km)	3¼hrs	1–2	108
18	Blencarn	Blencarn	10¼ miles (16.6km)	5¾hrs	4	113
19	Little Salkeld Watermill	Little Salkeld Watermill	5½ miles (8.7km)	2½hrs	1–2	118
20	Melmerby village	Melmerby village	8¾ miles (14.2km)	5hrs	4	124
21	Renwick	Renwick	10 miles (16km)	5hrs	2	129
22	Armathwaite	Armathwaite	3½ miles (5.8km)	1½hrs	1–2	135
23	Croglin	Croglin	5 miles (8km)	2¾hrs	2	138
24	Wetheral station	Armathwaite station	8½ miles (13.9km)	4¼hrs	2	142
25	Talkin	Talkin	6¼ miles (10.1km)	3¾hrs	2–3	148
26	Talkin Tarn	Talkin Tarn	7¾ miles (12.6km)	4½hrs	2	153
27	Lanercost Bridge	Lanercost Bridge	4 miles (6.4km)	2hrs	1–2	159
28	Bitts Park, Carlisle	Rockcliffe Primary School	8 miles (12.9km)	4¼hrs	1–2	165
29	Burgh by Sands	Burgh by Sands	7 miles (11.3km)	3hrs	1–2	173
30	Rockcliffe	Rockcliffe	7½ miles (12.1km)	3¼hrs	1–2	179

APPENDIX B
Useful contacts

Tourist Information Centres
Carlisle
Old Town Hall
Green Market
Carlisle
CA3 8JH
Tel. 01228 625 600

Brampton
Moot Hall
Market Place
Brampton
CA8 1RW
Tel. 016977 3433

Appleby
Moot Hall
Boroughgate
Appleby
CA16 6XE
Tel. 017683 54206
www.visiteden.co.uk

Kirkby Stephen
Market Place
Kirkby Stephen
CA17 4QN
Tel. 017683 71199
www.visiteden.co.uk

Penrith
Middlegate
Penrith
CA11 7PT
Tel. 01768 867466
www.visiteden.co.uk

Other useful sources of information
Access restrictions
www.naturalengland.org.uk

Traveline
Tel. 0871 200 2233
www.traveline.org.uk

Settle–Carlisle Railway
www.settle-carlisle.co.uk

Mountain Weather Information Service
www.mwis.org.uk

Acorn Bank Garden and Watermill
Tel. 01768 361893
www.nationaltrust.org.uk

Brougham Castle
Tel. 01768 862488
www.english-heritage.org.uk

Carlisle Castle
Tel. 01228 591922
www.english-heritage.org.uk

Clifton Hall
www.english-heritage.org.uk

Lanercost Priory
Tel. 01697 73030
www.english-heritage.org.uk

Cumbria Wildlife Trust
www.cumbriawildlifetrust.org.uk

Eden Rivers Trust
www.edenriverstrust.org.uk

NOTES

NOTES

LISTING OF CICERONE GUIDES

The GR5 Trail
The Robert Louis Stevenson
 Trail
Tour of the Oisans: The GR54
Tour of the Queyras
Tour of the Vanoise
Trekking in the Vosges and
 Jura
Vanoise Ski Touring
Walking in Provence
Walking in the Cathar Region
Walking in the Cevennes
Walking in the Dordogne
Walking in the Haute Savoie
 North & South
Walking in the Languedoc
Walking in the Tarentaise and
 Beaufortain Alps
Walking on Corsica

GERMANY
Germany's Romantic Road
Walking in the Bavarian Alps
Walking in the Harz
 Mountains
Walking the River Rhine Trail

HIMALAYA
Annapurna: A Trekker's
 Guide
Bhutan
Everest: A Trekker's Guide
Garhwal and Kumaon: A
 Trekker's and Visitor's
 Guide
Kangchenjunga: A Trekker's
 Guide
Langtang with Gosainkund
 and Helambu: A Trekker's
 Guide
Manaslu: A Trekker's Guide
The Mount Kailash Trek

IRELAND
Irish Coastal Walks
The Irish Coast to Coast Walk
The Mountains of Ireland

ITALY
Gran Paradiso
Italy's Sibillini National Park
Shorter Walks in the
 Dolomites

Through the Italian Alps
Trekking in the Apennines
Trekking in the Dolomites
Via Ferratas of the Italian
 Dolomites: Vols 1 & 2
Walking in Sicily
Walking in the Central Italian
 Alps
Walking in the Dolomites
Walking in Tuscany
Walking on the Amalfi Coast

MEDITERRANEAN
Jordan – Walks, Treks,
 Caves, Climbs and Canyons
The Ala Dag
The High Mountains of Crete
The Mountains of Greece
Treks and Climbs in Wadi
 Rum, Jordan
Walking in Malta
Western Crete

NORTH AMERICA
British Columbia
The Grand Canyon
The John Muir Trail
The Pacific Crest Trail

SOUTH AMERICA
Aconcagua and the Southern
 Andes
Torres del Paine

SCANDINAVIA
Trekking in Greenland
Walking in Norway

SLOVENIA, CROATIA AND
MONTENEGRO
The Julian Alps of Slovenia
The Mountains of Montenegro
Trekking in Slovenia
Walking in Croatia

SPAIN AND PORTUGAL
Costa Blanca Walks
 1 West & 2 East
Mountain Walking in
 Southern Catalunya
The Mountains of Central
 Spain
Trekking through Mallorca
Via de la Plata

Walking in Madeira
Walking in Mallorca
Walking in the Algarve
Walking in the Canary Islands
 2 East
Walking in the Cordillera
 Cantabrica
Walking in the Sierra Nevada
Walking on La Gomera and
 El Hierro
Walking on La Palma
Walking the GR7 in
 Andalucia
Walks and Climbs in the
 Picos de Europa

SWITZERLAND
Alpine Pass Route
Central Switzerland
The Bernese Alps
Tour of the Jungfrau Region
Walking in the Valais
Walking in Ticino
Walks in the Engadine

TECHNIQUES
Geocaching in the UK
Indoor Climbing
Lightweight Camping
Map and Compass
Mountain Weather
Moveable Feasts
Rock Climbing
Sport Climbing
The Book of the Bivvy
The Hillwalker's Guide to
 Mountaineering
The Hillwalker's Manual

MINI GUIDES
Avalanche!
Navigating with a GPS
Navigation
Pocket First Aid and
 Wilderness Medicine
Snow

For full information on all our
guides, and to order books
and eBooks, visit our website:
www.cicerone.co.uk.

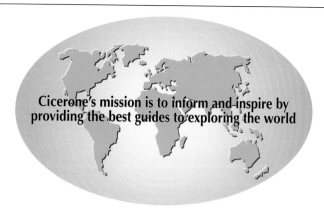

Cicerone's mission is to inform and inspire by providing the best guides to exploring the world

Since its foundation 40 years ago, Cicerone has specialised in publishing guidebooks and has built a reputation for quality and reliability. It now publishes nearly 300 guides to the major destinations for outdoor enthusiasts, including Europe, UK and the rest of the world.

Written by leading and committed specialists, Cicerone guides are recognised as the most authoritative. They are full of information, maps and illustrations so that the user can plan and complete a successful and safe trip or expedition – be it a long face climb, a walk over Lakeland fells, an alpine cycling tour, a Himalayan trek or a ramble in the countryside.

With a thorough introduction to assist planning, clear diagrams, maps and colour photographs to illustrate the terrain and route, and accurate and detailed text, Cicerone guides are designed for ease of use and access to the information.

If the facts on the ground change, or there is any aspect of a guide that you think we can improve, we are always delighted to hear from you.

Cicerone Press
2 Police Square Milnthorpe Cumbria LA7 7PY
Tel: 015395 62069 Fax: 015395 63417
info@cicerone.co.uk www.cicerone.co.uk